The Warren Buffett Portfolio

Mastering the Power of the Focus Investment Strategy

ROBERT G. HAGSTROM

JOHN WILEY & SONS, INC.

New York • Chichester • Weinheim • Brisbane • Singapore • Toronto

This book is printed on acid-free paper. ∞

Copyright © 1999 by Robert G. Hagstrom. All rights reserved.

Published by John Wiley & Sons, Inc.
Published simultaneously in Canada.

No part of this publication may be reproduced, stored in a retrieval system or
transmitted in any form or by any means, electronic, mechanical, photocopying,
recording, scanning or otherwise, except as permitted under Section 107 or 108 of
the 1976 United States Copyright Act, without either the prior written permission
of the Publisher, or authorization through payment of the appropriate per-copy fee
to the Copyright Clearance Center, 222 Rosewood Drive, Danvers, MA 01923,
(978) 750-8400, fax (978) 750-4744. Requests to the Publisher for permission
should be addressed to the Permissions Department, John Wiley & Sons, Inc.,
605 Third Avenue, New York, NY 10158-0012, (212) 850-6011, fax (212) 850-6008,
E-Mail: PERMREQ@WILEY.COM.

This publication is designed to provide accurate and authoritative information in
regard to the subject matter covered. It is sold with the understanding that the
publisher is not engaged in rendering professional services. If professional advice
or other expert assistance is required, the services of a competent professional
person should be sought.

Library of Congress Cataloging-in-Publication Data:

ISBN 0-471-24766-9

Printed in the United States of America.

10 9 8 7 6 5 4 3 2 1

To Bob and Ruth Hagstrom,
who with love, patience, and support
allowed their son to find his own path.

PREFACE

With *The Warren Buffett Way,* my goal was to outline the investment tools, or tenets, that Warren Buffett employs to select common stocks, so that ultimately readers would be able to thoughtfully analyze a company and purchase its stock as Buffett would.

The book's remarkable success is reasonable proof that our work was helpful. With over 600,000 copies in print, including twelve foreign-language translations, I am confident the book has endured sufficient scrutiny by professional and individual investors as well as academicians and business owners. To date, feedback from readers and the media has been overwhelmingly positive. The book appears to have genuinely helped people invest more intelligently.

As I have said on many occasions, the success of *The Warren Buffett Way* is first and foremost a testament to Warren Buffett. His wit and integrity have charmed millions of people worldwide, and his intellect and investment record have, for years, mesmerized the professional investment community, me included. It is an unparalleled combination that makes Warren Buffett the single most popular role model in investing today.

This new book, *The Warren Buffett Portfolio,* is meant to be a companion, not a sequel, to *The Warren Buffett Way.* In the original work, I unwittingly passed lightly over two important areas: structure and cognition—or, in simpler terms, portfolio management and intellectual fortitude.

I now realize more powerfully than ever that achieving above-average returns is not only a matter of which stocks you pick but also how you structure your portfolio. To successfully navigate a focus portfolio, you need to acquire a higher-level understanding of price volatility and its effect on individual behavior, and you need a certain kind of personal temperament. All these ideas come together in *The Warren Buffett Portfolio.*

The two companion books fit together this way: *The Warren Buffett Way* gives you tools that help you pick common stocks wisely, and *The Warren Buffett Portfolio* shows you how to organize them into a focus portfolio and provides the intellectual framework for managing it.

Since writing *The Warren Buffett Way,* all of my investments have been made according to the tenets outlined in the book. Indeed, the Legg Mason Focus Trust, the mutual fund that I manage, is a laboratory example of the book's recommendations. To date, I am happy to report, the results have been very encouraging.

Over the past four years, in addition to gaining experience managing a focus portfolio, I have had the opportunity to learn several more valuable lessons, which I describe here. Buffett believes that it is very important to have a fundamental grasp of mathematics and probabilities, and that investors should understand the psychology of the market. He warns us against the dangers of relying on market forecasting. However, his tutelage has been limited in each of these areas. We have an ample body of work to analyze how he picks stocks, but Buffett's public statements describing probabilities, psychology, and forecasting are comparatively few.

This does not diminish the importance of the lessons; it simply means I have been forced to fill in the blank spaces with my own interpretations and the interpretations of others. In this pursuit, I have relied on mathematician Ed Thorp, PhD, to help me better understand probabilities; Charlie Munger, to help me appreciate the psychology of misjudgment; and Bill Miller, to educate me about the science of complex adaptive systems.

A few general comments about the structure of the book are in order. Imagine two large, not quite symmetrical segments, bracketed by an introductory chapter and a conclusion. The first chapter previews, in summary fashion, the concept of focus investing and its main elements. Chapters 2 through 5 constitute the first large segment. Taken together, they present both the academic and the statistical rationales for focus investing, and they explore the lessons to be learned from the experiences of well-known focus investors.

We are interested not only in the intellectual framework that supports focus investing but also in the behavior of focus portfolios in general. Unfortunately, until now, the historical database of focus portfolios has contained too few observations to draw any statistically meaningful conclusions. An exciting new body of research has the potential to change that.

For the past two years, Joan Lamm-Tennant, PhD, and I have conducted a research study on the theory and process of focus investing. In the study, we took an in-depth look at 3,000 focus portfolios over different time periods, and then compared the behavior of these portfolios to the sort of broadly diversified portfolios that today dominate mutual funds and institutional accounts. The results are formally presented in an academic monograph titled "Focus Investing: An Optimal Portfolio Strategy Alternative to Active versus Passive Management," and what we discovered is summarized, in nonacademic language, in Chapter 4.

In Chapters 6 through 8, the second large segment of the book, we turn our attention to other fields of study: mathematics, psychology, and the new science of complexity. You will find here the new ideas that I have learned from Ed Thorp, Charlie

Munger, and Bill Miller. Some people may think it strange that we are venturing into apparently unrelated areas. But I believe that without the understanding gained from these other disciplines, any attempt at focus investing will stumble.

Finally, Chapter 9 gives consolidated information about the characteristics of focus investors, along with clear guidance so that you can initiate a focus investment strategy for your own portfolio.

ROBERT G. HAGSTROM

Wayne, Pennsylvania
February 1999

CONTENTS

Contents

ONE

Focus Investing

Robert, we just focus on a few outstanding companies.
We're focus investors.

—Warren Buffett

I REMEMBER THAT conversation with Warren Buffett as if it happened yesterday. It was for me a defining moment, for two reasons. First, it moved my thinking in a totally new direction; and second, it gave a name to an approach to portfolio management that I instinctively felt made wonderful sense but that our industry had long overlooked. That approach is what we now call focus investing, and it is the exact opposite of what most people imagine that experienced investors do.

Hollywood has given us a visual cliché of a money manager at work: talking into two phones at once, frantically taking notes while trying to keep an eye on jittery computer screens that blink and blip from all directions, slamming the keyboard whenever one of those computer blinks shows a minuscule drop in stock price.

Warren Buffett, the quintessential focus investor, is as far from that stereotype of frenzy as anything imaginable. The man

1

whom many consider the world's greatest investor is usually described with words like "soft-spoken," "down-to-earth," and "grandfatherly." He moves with the calm that is born of great confidence, yet his accomplishments and his performance record are legendary. It is no accident that the entire investment industry pays close attention to what he does. If Buffett characterizes his approach as "focus investing," we would be wise to learn what that means and how it is done.

Focus investing is a remarkably simple idea, and yet, like most simple ideas, it rests on a complex foundation of interlocking concepts. If we hold the idea up to the light and look closely at all its facets, we find depth, substance, and solid thinking below the bright clarity of the surface.

In this book, we will look closely at these interlocking concepts, one at a time. For now, I hope merely to introduce you to the core notion of focus investing. The goal of this overview chapter mirrors the goal of the book: to give you a new way of thinking about investment decisions and managing investment portfolios. Fair warning: this new way is, in all likelihood, the opposite of what you have always been told about investing in the stock market. It is as far from the usual way of thinking about stocks as Warren Buffett is from that Hollywood cliché.

The essence of focus investing can be stated quite simply:

> Choose a few stocks that are likely to produce above-average returns over the long haul, concentrate the bulk of your investments in those stocks, and have the fortitude to hold steady during any short-term market gyrations.

No doubt that summary statement immediately raises all sorts of questions in your mind:

How do I identify those above-average stocks?

How many is "a few"?

What do you mean by "concentrate"?

How long must I hold?

And, saved for last:

Why should I do this?

The full answers to those questions are found in the subsequent chapters. Our work here is to construct an overview of the focus process, beginning with the very sensible question of why you should bother.

PORTFOLIO MANAGEMENT TODAY: A CHOICE OF TWO

In its current state, portfolio management appears to be locked into a tug-of-war between two competing strategies: active portfolio management and index investing.

Active portfolio managers constantly buy and sell a great number of common stocks. Their job is to try to keep their clients satisfied, and that means consistently outperforming the market so that on any given day, if a client applies the obvious measuring stick—"How is my portfolio doing compared to the market overall?"—the answer is positive and the client leaves her money in the fund. To keep on top, active managers try to predict what will happen with stocks in the coming six months and continually churn the portfolio, hoping to take advantage of their predictions. On average, today's common stock mutual funds own more than one hundred stocks and generate turnover ratios of 80 percent.

Index investing, on the other hand, is a buy-and-hold passive approach. It involves assembling, and then holding, a broadly diversified portfolio of common stocks deliberately designed to mimic the behavior of a specific benchmark index, such as the Standard & Poor's 500 Price Index (S&P 500).

Compared to active management, index investing is somewhat new and far less common. Since the 1980s, when index funds fully came into their own as a legitimate alternative strategy, proponents of both approaches have waged combat to determine which one will ultimately yield the higher investment return. Active portfolio managers argue that, by virtue of their superior stock-picking skills, they can do better than any index. Index strategists, for their part, have recent history on their side. In a study that tracked results in a twenty-year period, from 1977 through 1997, the percentage of equity mutual funds that have been able to beat the S&P 500 dropped dramatically, from 50 percent in the early years to barely 25 percent in the last four years. Since 1997, the news is even worse. As of November 1998, 90 percent of actively managed funds were underperforming the market (averaging 14 percent *lower* than the S&P 500), which means that only 10 percent were doing better.[1]

Active portfolio management, as commonly practiced today, stands a very small chance of outperforming the S&P 500. Because they frenetically buy and sell hundreds of stocks each year, institutional money managers have, in a sense, become the market. Their basic theory is: Buy today whatever we predict can be sold soon at a profit, regardless of what it is. The fatal flaw in that logic is that, given the complex nature of the financial universe, predictions are impossible. (See Chapter 8 for a description of complex adaptive systems.) Further complicating this shaky theoretical foundation is the effect of the inherent costs that go with this high level of activity—costs that diminish the net returns to investors. When we factor in these costs, it becomes apparent that the active money management business has created its own downfall.

Indexing, because it does not trigger equivalent expenses, is better than actively managed portfolios in many respects. But even the best index fund, operating at its peak, will only net exactly the returns of the overall market. Index investors can do no worse than the market—and no better.

From the investor's point of view, the underlying attraction of both strategies is the same: minimize risk through diversification. By holding a large number of stocks representing many industries and many sectors of the market, investors hope to create a warm blanket of protection against the horrific loss that could occur if they had all their money in one arena that suffered some disaster. In a normal period (so the thinking goes), some stocks in a diversified fund will go down and others will go up, and let's keep our fingers crossed that the latter will compensate for the former. The chances get better, active managers believe, as the number of stocks in the portfolio grows; ten is better than one, and a hundred is better than ten.

An index fund, by definition, affords this kind of diversification if the index it mirrors is also diversified, as they usually are. The traditional stock mutual fund, with upward of a hundred stocks constantly in motion, also offers diversification.

We have all heard this mantra of *diversification* for so long, we have become intellectually numb to its inevitable consequence: mediocre results. Although it is true that active *and* index funds offer diversification, in general neither strategy will yield exceptional returns. These are the questions intelligent investors must ask themselves: Am I satisfied with average returns? Can I do better?

A NEW CHOICE

What does Warren Buffett say about this ongoing debate regarding index versus active strategy? Given these two particular choices, he would unhesitatingly pick indexing. Especially if he were thinking of investors with a very low tolerance for risk, and people who know very little about the economics of a business but still want to participate in the long-term benefits of investing in common stocks. "By periodically investing in an index fund," Buffett says in his inimitable style, "the know-nothing investor can actually outperform most investment professionals."[2]

Buffett, however, would be quick to point out that there is a third alternative, a very different kind of active portfolio strategy that significantly increases the odds of beating the index. That alternative is focus investing.

FOCUS INVESTING: THE BIG PICTURE

"Find Outstanding Companies"

Over the years, Warren Buffett has developed a way of choosing the companies he considers worthy places to put his money. His choice rests on a notion of great common sense: if the company itself is doing well and is managed by smart people, eventually its inherent value will be reflected in its stock price. Buffett thus devotes most of his attention not to tracking share price but to analyzing the economics of the underlying business and assessing its management.

This is not to suggest that analyzing the company—uncovering all the information that tells us its economic value—is particularly easy. It does indeed take some work. But Buffett has often remarked that doing this "homework" requires no more energy than is expended in trying to stay on top of the market, and the results are infinitely more useful.

The analytical process that Buffett uses involves checking each opportunity against a set of investment tenets, or fundamental principles. These tenets, presented in depth in *The Warren Buffett Way* and summarized on page 8, can be thought of as a kind of tool belt. Each individual tenet is one analytical tool, and, in the aggregate, they provide a method for isolating the companies with the best chance for high economic returns.

The Warren Buffett tenets, if followed closely, lead you inevitably to good companies that make sense for a focus portfolio. That is because you will have chosen companies with a long history of superior performance and a stable management, and that stability predicts a high probability of performing in the future as they have in the past. And that is the heart of focus investing: concentrating your investments in companies that have the highest probability of above-average performance.

Probability theory, which comes to us from the science of mathematics, is one of the underlying concepts that make up the rationale for focus investing. In Chapter 6, you will learn more about probability theory and how it applies to investing. For the moment, try the mental exercise of thinking of "good companies" as "high-probability events." Through your analysis, you have already identified companies with a good history and, therefore, good prospects for the future; now, take what you already know and think about it in a different way—in terms of probabilities.

"Less Is More"

Remember Buffett's advice to a "know-nothing" investor, to stay with index funds? What is more interesting for our purposes is what he said next:

Tenets of the Warren Buffett Way

Business Tenets

Is the business simple and understandable?

Does the business have a consistent operating history?

Does the business have favorable long-term prospects?

Management Tenets

Is management rational?

Is management candid with its shareholders?

Does management resist the institutional imperative?

Financial Tenets

Focus on return on equity, not earnings per share.

Calculate "owner earnings."

Look for companies with high profit margins.

For every dollar retained, make sure the company has created at least one dollar of market value.

Market Tenets

What is the value of the business?

Can the business be purchased at a significant discount to its value?

"If you are a know-something investor, able to understand business economics and to find five to ten sensibly priced companies that possess important long-term competitive advantages, conventional diversification [broadly based active portfolios] makes no sense for you."[3]

What's wrong with conventional diversification? For one thing, it greatly increases the chances that you will buy something you don't know enough about. "Know-something" investors, applying the Buffett tenets, would do better to focus their attention on just a few companies—"five to ten," Buffett suggests. Others who adhere to the focus philosophy have suggested smaller numbers, even as low as three; for the average investor, a legitimate case can be made for ten to fifteen. Thus, to the earlier question, How many is "a few"? the short answer is: No more than fifteen. More critical than determining the exact number is understanding the general concept behind it. Focus investing falls apart if it is applied to a large portfolio with dozens of stocks.

Warren Buffett often points to John Maynard Keynes, the British economist, as a source of his ideas. In 1934, Keynes wrote to a business associate: "It is a mistake to think one limits one's risks by spreading too much between enterprises about which one knows little and has no reason for special confidence. . . . One's knowledge and experience are definitely limited and there are seldom more than two or three enterprises at any given time in which I personally feel myself entitled to put full confidence."[4] Keynes's letter may be the first piece written about focus investing.

An even more profound influence was Philip Fisher, whose impact on Buffett's thinking has been duly noted. Fisher, a prominent investment counselor for nearly half a century, is the author of two important books: *Common Stocks and Uncommon Profits* and *Paths to Wealth Through Common Stocks,* both of which Buffett admires greatly.

Phil Fisher was known for his focus portfolios; he always said he preferred owning a small number of outstanding companies that he understood well to owning a large number of average ones, many of which he understood poorly. Fisher began his investment counseling business shortly after the 1929 stock market crash, and he remembers how important it was to produce good results. "Back then, there was no room for mistakes," he remembers. "I knew the more I understood about the company the better off I would be."[5] As a general rule, Fisher limited his portfolios to fewer than ten companies, of which three or four often represented 75 percent of the total investment.

"It never seems to occur to [investors], much less their advisors," he wrote in *Common Stocks* in 1958, "that buying a company without having sufficient knowledge of it may be even more dangerous than having inadequate diversification."[6] More than forty years later, Fisher, who today is ninety-one, has not changed his mind. "Great stocks are extremely hard to find," he told me. "If they weren't, then everyone would own them. I knew I wanted to own the best or none at all."[7]

Ken Fisher, the son of Phil Fisher, is also a successful money manager. He summarizes his father's philosophy this way: "My dad's investment approach is based on an unusual but insightful notion that less is more."[8]

"Put Big Bets on High-Probability Events"

Fisher's influence on Buffett can also be seen in his belief that when you encounter a strong opportunity, the only reasonable course is to make a large investment. Like all great investors, Fisher was very disciplined. In his drive to understand as much as possible about a company, he made countless field trips to visit companies he was interested in. If he liked what he saw, he did not hesitate to invest a significant amount of money in the company. Ken Fisher points out, "My dad saw what it meant to have a large position in something that paid off."[9]

Today, Warren Buffett echoes that thinking: "With each investment you make, you should have the courage and the conviction to place at least 10 percent of your net worth in that stock."[10]

You can see why Buffett says the ideal portfolio should contain no more than ten stocks, if each is to receive 10 percent. Yet focus investing is not a simple matter of finding ten good stocks and dividing your investment pool equally among them. Even though all the stocks in a focus portfolio are high-probability events, some will inevitably be higher than others and should be allocated a greater proportion of the investment.

Blackjack players understand this tactic intuitively: When the odds are strongly in your favor, put down a big bet. In the eyes of many pundits, investors and gamblers have much in common, perhaps because both draw from the same science: mathematics. Along with probability theory, mathematics provides another piece of the focus investing rationale: the Kelly Optimization Model. The Kelly model is represented in a formula that uses probability to calculate optimization—in this case, optimal investment proportion. (The model, along with the fascinating story of how it was originally derived, is presented in Chapter 6.)

I cannot say with certainty whether Warren Buffett had optimization theory in mind when he bought American Express stock in late 1963, but the purchase is a clear example of the concept— and of Buffett's boldness. During the 1950s and 1960s, Buffett served as general partner in a limited investment partnership in Omaha, Nebraska, where he still lives. The partnership was allowed to take large positions in the portfolio when profitable opportunities arose, and, in 1963, one such opportunity came along.

During the infamous Tino de Angelis salad oil scandal, the American Express share price dropped from $65 to $35 when it was thought the company would be held liable for millions of dollars of fraudulent warehouse receipts. Warren invested $13 million—a whopping 40 percent of his partnership's assets—in ownership of close to 5 percent of the shares outstanding of American Express. Over the next two years, the share price tripled, and the Buffett partnership walked away with a $20 million profit.

"Be Patient"

Focus investing is the antithesis of a broadly diversified, high-turnover approach. Among all active strategies, focus investing stands the best chance of outperforming an index return over time, but it requires investors to patiently hold their portfolio even when it appears that other strategies are marching ahead. In shorter periods, we realize that changes in interest rates, inflation, or the near-term expectation for a company's earnings can affect share prices. But as the time horizon lengthens, the trend-line economics of the underlying business will increasingly dominate its share price.

How long is that ideal time line? As you might imagine, there is no hard and fast rule (although Buffett would probably say that any span shorter than five years is a fool's theory). The goal is not zero turnover; that would be foolish in the opposite direction because it would prevent you from taking advantage of something better when it comes along. I suggest that, as a general rule of thumb, we should be thinking of a turnover rate between 10 and 20 percent. A 10 percent turnover rate suggests that you would hold the stock for ten years, and a 20 percent rate implies a five-year period.

"Don't Panic over Price Changes"

Price volatility is a necessary by-product of focus investing. In a traditional active portfolio, broad diversification has the effect of averaging out the inevitable shifts in the prices of individual stocks. Active portfolio managers know all too well what happens when investors open their monthly statement and see, in cold black and white, a drop in the dollar value of their holdings. Even those who understand intellectually that such dips are part of the normal course of events may react emotionally and fall into panic.

The more diversified the portfolio, the less the chances that any one share-price change will tilt the monthly statement. It is indeed true that broad diversification is a source of great comfort to many investors because it smooths out the bumps along the way. It is also true that a smooth ride is flat. When, in the interests of avoiding unpleasantness, you average out all the ups and downs, what you get is average results.

Focus investing pursues *above*-average results. As we will see in Chapter 3, there is strong evidence, both in academic research and actual case histories, that the pursuit is successful. There can be no doubt, however, that the ride is bumpy. Focus investors tolerate the bumpiness because they know that, in the long run, the underlying economics of the companies will more than compensate for any short-term price fluctuations.

Buffett is a master bump ignorer. So is his longtime friend and colleague Charlie Munger, the vice chairman of Berkshire Hathaway. The many fans who devour Berkshire's remarkable annual reports know that the two men support and reinforce each other with complementary and sometimes indistinguishable ideas. Munger's attitudes and philosophy have influenced Buffett every bit as much as Buffett has influenced Munger.

In the 1960s and 1970s, Munger ran an investment partnership in which, like Buffett at about the same time, he had the freedom to make big bets in the portfolio. His intellectual reasoning for his decisions during those years echoes the principles of focus investing.

"Back in the 1960s, I actually took a compound interest rate table," explained Charlie, "and I made various assumptions about what kind of edge I might have in reference to the behavior of common stocks generally." (OID)[11] Charlie worked through several scenarios, including the number of stocks he would need in the portfolio and what kind of volatility he could expect. It was a straightforward calculation.

"I knew from being a poker player that you have to bet heavily when you've got huge odds in your favor," Charlie said. He concluded that as long as he could handle the price volatility, owning as few as three stocks would be plenty. "I knew I could handle the bumps psychologically," he said, "because I was raised by people who believe in handling bumps. So I was an ideal person to adopt my own methodology." (OID)[12]

Maybe you also come from a long line of people who can handle bumps. But even if you were not born so lucky, you can acquire some of their traits. The first step is to consciously decide to change how you think and behave. Acquiring new habits and thought patterns does not happen overnight, but gradually teaching yourself not to panic and not to act rashly in response to the vagaries of the market is certainly doable.

You may find some comfort in learning more about the psychology of investing (see Chapter 7); social scientists, working in a field called behavioral finance, have begun to seriously investigate the psychological aspects of the investment phenomenon. You may also find it helpful to use a different measuring stick for evaluating success. If watching stock prices fall gives you heart failure, perhaps it is time to embrace another way of measuring performance, a way that is less immediately piercing but equally valid (*even more valid,* Buffett would say). That new measurement involves the concept of economic benchmarking, presented in Chapter 4.

Focus investing, as we said earlier, is a simple idea that draws its vigor from several interconnecting principles of logic, mathematics, and psychology. With the broad overview of those principles that has been introduced in this chapter, we can now rephrase the basic idea, using wording that incorporates concrete guidelines.

In summary, the process of focus investing involves these actions:

- Using the tenets of the Warren Buffett Way, choose a few (ten to fifteen) outstanding companies that have achieved above-average returns in the past and that you believe have a high probability of continuing their past strong performance into the future.
- Allocate your investment funds proportionately, placing the biggest bets on the highest-probability events.
- As long as things don't deteriorate, leave the portfolio largely intact for at least five years (longer is better), and teach yourself to ride through the bumps of price volatility with equanimity.

A LATTICEWORK OF MODELS

Warren Buffett did not invent focus investing. The fundamental rationale was originally articulated more than fifty years ago by

John Maynard Keynes. What Buffett did, with stunning success, was apply the rationale, even before he gave it its name. The question that fascinates me is why Wall Street, noted for its unabashed willingness to copy success, has so far disregarded focus investing as a legitimate approach.

In 1995, we launched Legg Mason Focus Trust, only the second mutual fund to purposely own fifteen (or fewer) stocks. (The first was Sequoia Fund; its story is told in Chapter 3.) Focus Trust has given me the invaluable experience of managing a focus portfolio. Over the past four years, I have had the opportunity to interact with shareholders, consultants, analysts, other portfolio managers, and the financial media, and what I have learned has led me to believe that focus investors operate in a world far different from the one that dominates the investment industry. The simple truth is, they *think* differently.

Charlie Munger helped me to understand this pattern of thinking by using the very powerful metaphor of a latticework of models. In 1995, Munger delivered a lecture entitled "Investment Expertise as a Subdivision of Elementary, Worldly Wisdom" to Professor Guilford Babcock's class at the University of Southern California School of Business. The lecture, which was covered in OID, was particularly fun for Charlie because it centered around a topic that he considers especially important: how people achieve true understanding, or what he calls "worldly wisdom."

A simple exercise of compiling and quoting facts and figures is not enough. Rather, Munger explains, wisdom is very much about how facts align and combine. He believes that the only way to achieve wisdom is to be able to hang life's experience across a broad cross-section of mental models. "You've got to have models in your head," he explained, "and you've got to array your experience—both vicarious and direct—on this latticework of models." (OID)[13]

The first rule to learn, says Charlie, is that you must carry multiple models in your mind. Not only do you need more than a few, but you need to embrace models from several different disciplines. Becoming a successful investor, he explains, requires a multidiscipline approach to your thinking.

That approach will put you in a different place from almost everyone else, Charlie points out, because the world is not multidiscipline. Business professors typically don't include physics in their lectures, and physics teachers don't include biology, and biology teachers don't include mathematics, and mathematicians rarely include psychology in their coursework. According to Charlie, we must ignore these "intellectual jurisdictional boundaries" and include all models in our latticework design.

"I think it is undeniably true that the human brain must work in models," says Charlie. "The trick is to have your brain work better than the other person's brain because it understands the most fundamental models—the ones that will do the most work per unit."

It is clear to me that focus investing does not fit neatly within the narrowly constructed models popularized and used in our investment culture. To receive the full benefit of the focus approach, we will have to add a few more concepts, a few more models, to our thinking. You will never be content with investing until you understand the behavior models that come from psychology. You will not know how to optimize a portfolio without learning the model of statistical probabilities. And it is likely you will never appreciate the folly of predicting markets until you understand the model of complex adaptive systems.

This investigation need not be overwhelming. "You don't have to become a huge expert in any one of these fields," explains Charlie. "All you have to do is take the really big ideas and learn them early and learn them well." (OID)[14] The exciting part to this exercise, Charlie points out, is the insight that is possible when several models combine and begin operating in the same direction.

The most detailed model that focus investors have to learn is the model for picking stocks, and many of you are already familiar with that from *The Warren Buffett Way*. From here, we need to add just a few more simple models to complete our education: to understand how to assemble those stocks into a portfolio, and how to manage that portfolio so that it yields maximum results well into the future. But we are not alone. We have Warren's and Charlie's wisdom to guide us, and we have their accumulated experience at Berkshire Hathaway. Typically, these two visionaries credit not themselves personally but their organization, which they describe as a "didactic enterprise teaching the right systems of thought, of which the chief lessons are that a few big ideas really work." (OID)[15]

"Berkshire is basically a very old-fashioned kind of place," Charlie Munger said, "and we try to exert discipline to stay that way. I don't mean old-fashioned stupid. I mean the eternal verities: basic mathematics, basic horse sense, basic fear, basic diagnosis of human nature making possible predictions regarding human behavior. If you just do that with a certain amount of discipline, I think it's likely to work out quite well." (OID)[16]

TWO

The High Priests of Modern Finance

Traditional wisdom can be long on tradition and short on wisdom.

—Warren Buffett

T HE WORST FINANCIAL disaster of the twentieth century was the stock market crash of 1929 and the Great Depression that followed it. The second worst was the bear market and recession of 1973–1974. It did not begin with a single horrific day, as did the 1929 crash, and its effects on American families were not so widespread nor so devastating, and so it does not hold the same place in our collective memory. Yet, for finance professionals, the second period is almost as important, for it represents a very important watershed in the history of modern finance and, particularly in the development of modern portfolio theory.

Looking back now with the clarity of hindsight, we can see that two very different schools of thought, which today still engage in serious debate about investment philosophy, had their beginnings during this two-year debacle. Two separate groups of people in the investment world searched for the best way to respond, and arrived at different conclusions. Actually, rather than describe them as two groups, it's probably more accurate to say that the searchers were one man—Warren Buffett—and one group—everybody else.

The bear market of 1973–1974 was a slow, tortuous process of unrelenting losses that lasted, uninterrupted, for two years. The broader markets declined by over 60 percent. Fixed-income holders who owned lower-coupon bonds saw their investments shrink. Interest rates and inflation soared to double digits. Oil prices skyrocketed. Mortgage rates were so high that very few middle-income families could afford to buy a new home. It was a dark, brutal time. So severe was the financial damage that investment managers began to question their own approach.

Looking for answers, most of the investment professionals gradually turned—some of them with great reluctance—to a body of academic study that had been largely ignored for two decades. Collectively, those academic studies have come to be called modern portfolio theory.

Buffett turned in a different direction.

Warren Buffett, the son of a stockbroker, began marking the board at his father's Omaha, Nebraska, firm when he was eleven years old. He bought his first shares of stock the same year. As a student at the University of Nebraska, the young man with a gift for numbers happened upon a book entitled *The Intelligent Investor*, by Benjamin Graham, a Columbia University professor. Graham believed that the critical piece of investment information is a company's intrinsic value. The core task for investors is to accurately calculate this value and then maintain the discipline to buy stock only when the price is below the calculated amount. Buffett was so attracted to this mathematical approach that he attended Columbia for graduate school so that he could study under Graham.

After completing a master's degree in economics, Buffett returned home to Omaha and began working for his father, who by then owned a brokerage firm named Buffett Falk & Company. It was 1952. The young Buffett set to work practicing Ben Graham's investment techniques. Just as Graham had taught him, Buffett would consider purchasing stocks only when they were selling well below their calculated worth. In true Graham fashion, Buffett's interest really perked up when stock prices traded lower.

While working with his father, Warren Buffett remained in close contact with his mentor, and in 1954 Graham invited his former student to join him in New York, working with the Graham-Newman Corporation. After two years, Graham retired and Buffett returned to Nebraska. With seven limited partners and $100 of his own money, he began the investment partnership that a few years later would make the stunning American Express deal described in Chapter 1. He was twenty-five years old.

As general partner, Buffett had essentially free rein to invest the partnership's funds. In addition to minority holdings such as American Express, he sometimes bought controlling interests in companies, and in 1962, he began acquiring a struggling textile company called Berkshire Hathaway.

In 1969, a dozen years after it was established, Buffett closed the investment partnership. He had set an ambitious original goal—to outperform the Dow Jones Industrial Average by ten points each year—and he had done far better: not ten, but twenty-two points. Some of his original investors wanted to continue with another money manager, so Buffett asked his friend and Columbia classmate Bill Ruane to handle their money. Ruane said yes, and that was the beginning of Sequoia Fund. (See Chapter 3 for more on Ruane.)

Buffett took his portion of the partnership profits, bought more shares of Berkshire Hathaway, and eventually gained control. Then, for the next few years, he settled down to managing the textile company.

PORTFOLIO MANAGEMENT THROUGH DIVERSIFICATION

In March 1952, about the time recent college graduate Warren Buffett went to work for his father's brokerage firm, there appeared in *The Journal of Finance* an article entitled "Portfolio Selection," by Harry Markowitz, a University of Chicago graduate student. It was not long—only fourteen pages—and, by the standards of academic journals, it was unremarkable: only four pages of text (graphs and mathematical equations consumed the rest) and only three citations. Yet that brief article is today credited with launching modern finance.[1]

From Markowitz's standpoint, it didn't take volumes to explain what he believed was a rather simple notion: return and risk are inextricably linked. As an economist, he believed it was possible to quantify the relationship between the two to a statistically valid degree, and thus determine the degree of risk that would be required for various levels of return. In his paper, he presented the calculations that supported his conclusion: no investor can achieve above-average gains without assuming above-average risk.

"I was struck with the notion that you should be interested in risk as well as return," Markowitz later remarked.[2] Although today this statement appears amazingly self-evident in light of what we have learned about investing, it was a revolutionary concept in the 1950s. Until that time, investors gave very little thought to managing a portfolio or to the concept of risk. Portfolios were constructed haphazardly. If a manager thought a stock was going to go up in price, it was simply added to the portfolio. No other thinking was required.

That puzzled Markowitz. Surely it was foolish, he reasoned, to believe that you can generate high returns without exposing yourself to some kind of risk. To help clarify his thoughts, Markowitz devised what he called the *efficient frontier.*

"Being an economist," he explained, "I drew a trade-off graph with the expected return on one axis and risk on the other axis."[3] The efficient frontier is simply a line drawn from the bottom left to the top right. Each point on that line represents an intersection between potential reward and its corresponding level of risk. The most efficient portfolio is the one that gives the highest return for a given level of portfolio risk. An inefficient portfolio is one that exposes the investor to a level of risk without a corresponding level of return. The goal for investment managers, said Markowitz, is to match portfolios to an investor's level of risk tolerance while limiting or avoiding inefficient portfolios.

In 1959, Markowitz published his first book, *Portfolio Selection: Efficient Diversification of Investment,* based on his PhD dissertation. In it, he described more thoroughly his ideas about risk. "I used standard deviation as a measure of risk," Markowitz explains. Variance (deviation) can be thought of as the distance from the average; according to Markowitz, the greater the distance from the average, the greater the risk.

We might think the riskiness of a portfolio, as defined by Markowitz, is simply the weighted average variance of all the individual stocks in the portfolio. But this misses a crucial point. Although variance may provide a gauge to the riskiness of an individual stock, the average of two variances (or one hundred variances) will tell you very little about the riskiness of a two-stock (or a hundred-stock) portfolio. What Markowitz did was find a way to determine the riskiness of the entire portfolio. Many believe it is his greatest contribution.

He called it "covariance," based on the already established formula for the variance of the weighted sum. Covariance measures the direction of a group of stocks. We say that two stocks exhibit high covariance when their prices, for whatever reason, tend to move together. Conversely, low covariance describes two stocks that move in opposite directions. In Markowitz's thinking, the risk of a portfolio is not the variance of the individual stocks but the covariance of the holdings. The more they move in the same direction, the greater is the chance that economic shifts will drive them all down at the same time. By the same token, a portfolio composed of risky stocks might actually be a conservative selection if the individual stock prices move differently. Either way, Markowitz said, diversification is the key.

According to Markowitz, the appropriate action sequence for an investor is to first identify the level of risk he or she is comfortable handling, and then construct an efficient diversified portfolio of low covariance stocks.

Markowitz's book, like the original paper seven years earlier, was, for all practical purposes, soundly ignored by investment professionals.

A MATHEMATICAL DEFINITION OF RISK

About ten years after Markowitz's groundbreaking paper first appeared, a young PhD student named Bill Sharpe approached

Markowitz, who was then working on linear programming at the RAND Institute. Sharpe was in need of a dissertation topic, and one of his professors at UCLA had suggested tracking down Markowitz. Markowitz told Sharpe of his work in portfolio theory and the need for estimating countless covariances. Sharpe listened intently, then returned to UCLA.

The next year, in 1963, Sharpe's dissertation was published: "A Simplified Model of Portfolio Analysis." While fully acknowledging his reliance on Markowitz's ideas, Sharpe suggested a simpler method that would avoid the countless covariant calculations required by Markowitz.

It was Sharpe's contention that all securities bore a common relationship with some underlying base factor. This factor could be a stock market index, the gross national product (GNP), or some other price index, as long as it was the single most important influence on the behavior of the security. Using Sharpe's theory, an analyst would need only to measure the relationship of the security to the dominant base factor. It greatly simplified Markowitz's approach.

Let's look at common stocks. According to Sharpe, the base factor for stock prices—the single greatest influence on their behavior—was the stock market itself. (Also important but less influential were industry groups and unique characteristics about the stock itself.) If the stock price is more volatile than the market as a whole, then the stock will make the portfolio more variable and therefore more risky. Conversely, if the stock price is less volatile than the market, then adding this stock will make the portfolio less variable and less volatile. Now, the volatility of the portfolio could be determined easily by the simple weighted average volatility of the individual securities.

Sharpe's volatility measure was given a name—beta factor. Beta is described as the degree of correlation between two separate price movements: the market as a whole and the individual stock. Stocks that rise and fall in value exactly in line with the market are assigned a beta of 1.0. If a stock rises and falls twice as fast as the market, its beta is 2.0; if a stock's move is only 80 percent of the market's move, the beta is 0.8. Based solely on this information, we can ascertain the weighted average beta of the portfolio. The conclusion is that any portfolio with a beta greater than 1.0 will be more risky than the market, and a portfolio with a beta less than 1.0 will be less risky.

A year after publishing his dissertation on portfolio theory, Sharpe introduced a far-reaching concept called the Capital Asset Pricing Model (CAPM). It was a direct extension of his single-factor model for composing efficient portfolios. According to CAPM, stocks carry two distinct risks. One risk is simply the risk of being in the market, which Sharpe called "systemic risk." Systemic risk is "beta" and it cannot be diversified away. The second type, called "unsystemic risk," is the risk specific to a company's economic position. Unlike systemic risk, unsystemic risk *can* be diversified away by simply adding different stocks to the portfolio.

Peter Bernstein, the noted writer, researcher, and founding editor of *The Journal of Portfolio Management*, has spent considerable time with Sharpe and has studied his work in depth. Bernstein believes that Sharpe's research points out one "inescapable conclusion": "The efficient portfolio is the stock market itself. No other portfolio with equal risk can offer a higher expected return; no other portfolio with equal expected return will be less risky."[4] In other words, the Capital Asset Pricing Model says the market portfolio lies perfectly on Markowitz's efficient frontier.

In the space of one decade, two academicians had defined two important elements of what would later be called modern portfolio theory: Markowitz with his idea that the proper reward–risk balance depends on diversification, and Sharpe with his definition of risk. A third element—the efficient market theory—came from a young assistant professor of finance at the University of Chicago, Eugene Fama.

EFFICIENT MARKET THEORY

Although several other distinguished researchers have written about efficient markets, including MIT economist Paul Samuelson, Fama is most credited with developing a comprehensive theory of the behavior of the stock market.

Fama began studying the changes in stock prices in the early 1960s. An intense reader, he absorbed all the written work on stock market behavior then available, but it appears he was especially influenced by the French mathematician Benoit Mandelbrot. Mandelbrot, who developed fractal geometry, argued that because stock prices fluctuated so irregularly, they would never oblige any fundamental or statistical research; furthermore, the pattern of irregular price movements was bound to intensify, causing unexpectedly large and intense shifts.

Fama's PhD dissertation, "The Behavior of Stock Prices," was published in *The Journal of Business* in 1963 and later excerpted in *The Financial Analysts Journal* and *The Institutional Investor*. Fama, a relatively young newcomer, had definitely caught the attention of the finance community.

Fama's message was very clear: Stock prices are not predictable because the market is too efficient. In an efficient market, as information becomes available, a great many smart people (Fama called them "rational profit maximizers") aggressively apply that information in a way that causes prices to adjust instantaneously, before anyone can profit. Predictions about the future therefore have no place in an efficient market, because the share prices adjust too quickly.

Fama did admit that it is impossible to test empirically the idea of an efficient market. The alternative, he figured, was to identify trading systems or traders who could outperform the stock market. If such a group existed, the market was obviously not efficient. But if no one could demonstrate an ability to beat the market, then we could assume that prices reflect all available information and hence the market is efficient.

The intertwined threads of modern portfolio theory were of consuming interest to the theorists and researchers who developed them, but, throughout the 1950s and 1960s, Wall Street paid little attention. Peter Bernstein has suggested a reason: during this time, portfolio management was "uncharted territory." However, by 1974, this all changed.

Without question, the 1973–1974 bear market forced investment professionals to take seriously the writings coming from academia that promoted new methods to control risk. The self-inflicted financial wounds caused by decades of careless speculation were simply too deep to ignore. "The market disaster of 1974 convinced me that there had to be a better way to manage investment portfolios," Bernstein said. "Even if I could have convinced myself to turn my back on the theoretical structure that the academics were erecting, there was too much of it coming from major universities for me to accept the view of my colleagues that it was 'a lot of baloney.' "[5]

Thus, for the first time in history, our financial destiny rested not on Wall Street or in Washington, and not even in the hands of business owners. As we moved forward, the financial landscape would be defined by a group of university professors on whose doors the finance professionals had finally come knocking. From their ivory towers, they now became the new high priests of modern finance.

BUFFETT AND MODERN PORTFOLIO THEORY

Meanwhile, even as he concentrated his energies on the Berkshire Hathaway business, Warren Buffett was keeping a keen eye on the market. Whereas most investment professionals saw 1973–1974 as a period of debilitating losses, Buffett, the disciple of Ben Graham, saw only opportunity. And he knew when to act.

Buffett described his rationale for investing in *The Washington Post* at a Stanford Law School lecture. As featured in OID, "We bought The Washington Post Company at a valuation of $80 million back in 1974," Buffett later recalled. "If you'd asked any one of 100 analysts how much the company was worth when we were buying it, no one would have argued about the fact it was worth $400 million. Now, under the whole theory of beta and modern portfolio theory, we would have been doing something riskier buying stock for $40 million than we were buying it for $80 million, even though it's worth $400 million—because it would have had more volatility. With that, they've lost me."(OID)[6]

The purchase of the *Post* was a clear signal that Buffett was embarking on a course that would put him at odds with most other investment professionals. He also made it clear what he thought of the three main ingredients of modern portfolio theory: risk, diversification, and an efficient market.

BUFFETT ON RISK

Recall that in modern portfolio theory, risk is defined by the volatility of the share price. But throughout his career, Buffett has always perceived a drop in share prices as an opportunity to make additional money. If anything, a dip in price actually reduces the risk Buffett takes. He points out, "For owners of a business—and that's the way we think of shareholders—the academics' definition of risk is far off the mark, so much so that it produces absurdities."[7]

Buffett has a different definition of risk: the possibility of harm or injury. And that is a factor of the "intrinsic value risk" of the business, not the price behavior of the stock.[8] The real risk, Buffett says, is whether after-tax returns from an investment "will give him [an investor] at least as much purchasing power as he had to begin with, plus a modest rate of interest on that initial stake."[9] In Buffett's view, harm or injury comes from misjudging the four primary factors that determine the future profits of your investment (see box), plus the uncontrollable, unpredictable effect of taxes and inflation.

Risk, for Buffett, is inextricably linked to an investor's time horizon. If you buy a stock today, he explains, with the intention of selling it tomorrow, then you have entered into a risky transaction. The odds of predicting whether share prices will be up or down in a short period are no greater than the odds of predicting the toss of a coin; you will lose half of the time. However, says Buffett, if you extend your time horizon out to several years, the probability of its being a risky transaction declines meaningfully, assuming of course that you have made a sensible purchase. "If you asked me to assess the risk of buying Coca-Cola this morning and selling it tomorrow morning," Buffett says, "I'd say that that's a very risky transaction." (OID)[10] But, in Buffett's

---

Is It a Good Investment?

To ascertain the probability of achieving a return on your initial stake, Buffett encourages you to keep four primary factors clearly in mind:

1. The certainty with which the long-term economic characteristics of the business can be evaluated.
2. The certainty with which management can be evaluated, both as to its ability to realize the full potential of the business and to wisely employ its cash flows.
3. The certainty with which management can be counted on to channel the rewards from the business to the shareholders rather than to itself.
4. The purchase price of the business.[11]

---

way of thinking, buying Coca-Cola this morning and holding it for ten years, carries zero risk.

BUFFETT ON DIVERSIFICATION

Buffett's view on risk drives his diversification strategy; here too, his thinking is the polar opposite of modern portfolio theory. According to that theory, remember, the primary benefit of a broadly diversified portfolio is to mitigate the price volatility of the individual stocks. But if you are unconcerned with price volatility, as Buffett is, then you will also see portfolio diversification in a different light.

"The strategy we've adopted precludes our following standard diversification dogma," says Buffett. "Many pundits would therefore say the strategy must be riskier than that employed by a more conventional investor. We believe that a policy of portfolio concentration may well decrease risk if it raises, as it should, both the intensity with which an investor thinks about a business and the comfort level he must feel with its economic characteristics before buying into it."[12] That is, by purposely focusing on just a few select companies, you are better able to study them closely and understand their intrinsic value. The more knowledge you have about your company, the less risk you are likely to be taking.

"Diversification serves as protection against ignorance," explains Buffett. "If you want to make sure that nothing bad happens to you relative to the market, you should own everything. There is nothing wrong with that. It's a perfectly sound approach for somebody who doesn't know how to analyze businesses." In many ways, modern portfolio theory protects investors who have limited knowledge and understanding of how to value a business. But that protection comes with a price. According to Buffett, "It [modern portfolio theory] will tell you how to do average. But I think almost anybody can figure out how to do average in the fifth grade." (OID)[13]

BUFFETT ON THE
EFFICIENT MARKET THEORY

If the efficient market theory is correct, there is no possibility, except a random chance, that any person or group could outperform the market, and certainly no chance that the same person or group could consistently do so. Yet Buffett's performance record for the past twenty-five years is prima facie evidence that it *is* possible, especially when combined with the experience of several other bright individuals who also have beaten the market by following Buffett's lead. What does that say about the efficient market theory?

"Proponents of the theory have never seemed interested in discordant evidence," Buffett observed. "Apparently, a reluctance to recant, and thereby to demystify the priesthood, is not limited to theologians."

The reasons why the efficient market theory is not defensible can be easily summarized:

1. Investors are not always rational. According to the efficient market theory, investors, by using all available information, set rational prices in the marketplace. However, extensive research in behavioral psychology suggests that investors do not possess rational expectations.
2. Investors do not process information correctly. They continually rely on shortcuts to determine stock prices, rather than the fundamental analysis that would reveal the intrinsic value of a company.
3. Performance yardsticks emphasize short-term performance, which makes it all but impossible to beat the market over the long term.

Buffett's problem with the efficient market theory rests on one central point: it makes no provision for investors who analyze all the available information and gain a competitive advantage by doing so. "Observing correctly that the market was frequently efficient, they went on to conclude incorrectly that it was *always* efficient. The difference between these propositions is night and day."[14]

Nonetheless, efficient market theory (EMT) is still religiously taught in business schools, a fact that gives Warren Buffett no end of satisfaction. "Naturally, the disservice done students and gullible investment professionals who have swallowed EMT has been an extraordinary service to us and other followers of Graham," Buffett wryly observed. "In any sort of a contest—financial, mental, or physical—it's an enormous advantage to have opponents who have been taught it's useless to even try. From a selfish standpoint, we should probably endow chairs to ensure the perpetual teaching of EMT."[15]

Modern theories notwithstanding, there *is* an investment strategy that is capable of outperforming the market, and it is guiding us toward an entirely new theory of portfolio management.

DEVELOPING A NEW PORTFOLIO THEORY

Today, investors are caught at an intellectual crossroad. To the left lies the pathway of modern portfolio theory. It assumes that investors are rational, the market is efficient, risk is defined by price volatility, and the only way to reduce risk is to diversify broadly. To the right lies the focus portfolio theory. It is distinctly separate and is grounded in this very different set of beliefs:

- Investors are not always rational; they suffer from periodic episodes of fear and greed.
- The market is not always efficient, and therefore investors willing to study and learn are given opportunities to beat the market.
- Risk is not price-based; it is economic-value–based.
- The optimal portfolio is a focus portfolio that stresses big bets on high-probability events, as opposed to equally weighted bets on a mixed bag of probabilities.

Before people can successfully use the focus portfolio strategy taught by Buffett, they must remove from their thinking the constructs of modern portfolio theory. Ordinarily, it would be easy to reject a model that is largely considered ineffectual; after all, there is nothing prideful or rewarding about being average. But modern portfolio theory has developed a long history and a deep culture. It is full of neat formulas and Nobel prize winners. We should not expect the defenders of modern portfolio theory to be easily swayed. To acquiesce threatens both their intellectual and financial capital.

Fortunately, we do not have to take on the task of dismantling modern portfolio theory. Unfolding events will take care of that. If we follow Buffett's advice, the success we earn will eventually work to overthrow the less-than-effective model. Although modern portfolio theory has its share of intellectual heavyweights, do not lose sight of the fact that the lineage of focus investing includes some of history's greatest investors: John Maynard Keynes, Phil Fisher, Charlie Munger, Lou Simpson, Bill Ruane, and Warren Buffett.

If you are ever thrown off balance by the rumblings of modern portfolio theorists, take heart in the advice Ben Graham gave to his students: "You are neither right nor wrong because the crowd disagrees with you. You are right because your data and reasoning are right."[16]

THREE

The Superinvestors of Buffettville

*Investing is not a game where the guy with the 160 IQ
beats the guy with the 130 IQ.*

—Warren Buffett

ABOUT HALFWAY THROUGH the high-flying 1920s, a
young Benjamin Graham, who was already beginning to
make his mark on Wall Street, approached Columbia University,
his alma mater, about teaching a night-school class in security
analysis. He had been thinking of writing a book on the subject,
and thought that teaching the class would help him organize his
ideas. Columbia accepted his proposal and put the class on the
schedule for the fall term of 1927.

No one was more surprised than Graham at the response. So
many people showed up that the school put guards at the door to
make sure those who were preregistered got their seats. Among
them was David L. Dodd, a young assistant professor from

Columbia's School of Business. He got in. The second year, the demand was even greater. Many attendees wanted to take the class over, in the hope of picking up new securities tips.

The following year was 1929. During the winter months, Graham was fully occupied in coping with the effects of the Crash, for himself and his clients, so work on the book was delayed. He had asked his former student, David Dodd, to help with the writing, but even so the groundbreaking book with the mild-mannered title *Security Analysis* did not appear until 1934—the height of the Great Depression. Graham later said the delay was providential, for it allowed him to include "wisdom acquired at the cost of much suffering."[1]

Security Analysis, universally acclaimed a classic, is still in print after five editions and sixty-five years. It is impossible to overstate its influence on the modern world of investing, or the enormous contributions of Ben Graham to the profession.

Fifty years after its original publication, the Columbia Business School sponsored a seminar marking the anniversary of this seminal text authored by two of its illustrious faculty. Warren Buffett, one of the school's best-known alumni and the most famous modern-day proponent of Graham's value approach, was invited to address the gathering.

Most of those in the audience that day in 1984—university professors, researchers, and other academicians, along with many investment professionals—still held firmly to modern portfolio theory and the validity of the efficient market. Buffett, as we know, just as firmly disagreed. In his speech, which he titled "The Superinvestors of Graham-and-Doddsville," Buffett told some stories, made a few unflashy jokes, and quietly but firmly demolished the platform on which rested the efficient market theory. It was a classic Warren Buffett delivery.[2]

He began by recapping the central argument of modern portfolio theory: the stock market is efficient, all stocks are priced correctly, and therefore anyone who beats the market year after year is simply lucky. Maybe so, he said, but I know some folks who have done it, and their success can't be explained away as simply random chance.

Still, to give the must-be-luck argument its fair hearing, he asked the audience to imagine a national coin-flipping contest in which 225 million Americans bet $1 on their guess. After each flip, the losers dropped out and the winners kept the pot and advanced to the next round. After ten events, Buffett explained, there would be 220,000 winners left who, by letting their winnings ride, would have gained $1,024. After another ten tosses, there would be 215 winners, each with $1 million.

Now, Buffett continued, the business school professors, analyzing this national contest, would point out that the coin tossers demonstrated no exceptional skill. The event could just as easily be replicated, they would protest, with a group of 225 million coin-flipping orangutans.

Slowly building his case, Buffett granted the statistical possibility that, by sheer chance, the orangutans might get the same results. But imagine, he asked his audience, if 40 of those 215 winning animals came from the same zoo. Wouldn't we want to ask the zookeeper what he feeds his now very rich orangutans?

The point, Buffett said, is that whenever a high concentration of *anything* occurs in one specific area, something unusual may be going on at that spot, and bears investigation. And what if—here comes his clincher—the members of this one unique group are defined not by where they live but by whom they learned from.

And thus we come to what Buffett called the "intellectual village" of Graham-and-Doddsville. All the examples he presented that day were centered on individuals who had managed to beat the market consistently over time—not because of luck, but because they all followed principles learned from the same source: Ben Graham.

Each of these investors called the flips differently, explained Buffett, but they are all linked by a common approach that seeks to take advantage of discrepancies between market price and intrinsic value. "Needless to say, our Graham and Dodd investors do not discuss beta, the Capital Asset Pricing Model, or covariance of returns," said Buffett. "These are not subjects of any interest to them. In fact, most of them would have trouble defining those terms."

In an article based on his 1984 speech, Buffett included tables that presented the impressive performance results of the residents of Graham-and-Doddsville.[3] Fifteen years later, I thought it might be interesting to take an updated look at a few people who exemplify the approach defined by Graham and who also share Buffett's belief in the value of a focused portfolio with a smaller number of stocks. I think of them as the Superinvestors of Buffettville: Charlie Munger, Bill Ruane, Lou Simpson, and, of course, Buffett himself. From their performance records there is much we can learn. But before we start this investigation, let us begin with the first focus investor.

JOHN MAYNARD KEYNES

Most people recognize John Maynard Keynes for his contributions to economic theory. In addition to being a great macroeconomic thinker, Keynes was a legendary investor. Proof of his investment prowess can be found in the performance record of the Chest Fund at King's College in Cambridge.

Prior to 1920, King's College investments were restricted to fixed-income securities. However, when Keynes was appointed the Second Bursar, in late 1919, he persuaded the trustees to begin a separate fund that would contain only common stocks, currency, and commodity futures. This separate account became the Chest Fund. From 1927, when he was named First Bursar, until his death in 1945, Keynes had sole responsibility for this account.

In 1934, the same year that *Security Analysis* was published, Keynes wrote the letter to a colleague (see Chapter 1) in which he explained why he preferred to limit his investments to just a few companies. Four years later, he prepared a full policy report for the Chest Fund, outlining his investment principles:

"**1.** A careful selection of a few investments having regard to their cheapness in relation to their probable actual and potential *intrinsic* [emphasis his] value over a period of years ahead and in relation to alternative investments at the time;

"**2.** A steadfast holding of these fairly large units through thick and thin, perhaps for several years, until either they have fulfilled their promise or it is evident that they were purchased on a mistake;

"**3.** A *balanced* [emphasis his] investment position, i.e, a variety of risks in spite of individual holdings being large, and if possible opposed risks."[4]

My reading of Keynes's investment policy suggests he was a focus investor. He purposely limited his stocks to a select few and relied on fundamental analysis to estimate the value of his picks relative to price. He liked to keep portfolio turnover at a very low rate. He recognized the importance of diversifying his risks. I believe that, to oppose risk, his strategy was to focus on high-quality predictable businesses with a variety of economic positions.

How well did Keynes perform? A quick study of Table 3.1 shows his stock selection and portfolio management skills were outstanding. During the eighteen-year period, the Chest Fund

Table 3.1   John Maynard Keynes

Year	Annual Percentage Change	
	Chest Fund (%)	U.K. Market (%)
1928	0.0	0.1
1929	0.8	6.6
1930	−32.4	−20.3
1931	−24.6	−25.0
1932	44.8	−5.8
1933	35.1	21.5
1934	33.1	−0.7
1935	44.3	5.3
1936	56.0	10.2
1937	8.5	−0.5
1938	−40.1	−16.1
1939	12.9	−7.2
1940	−15.6	−12.9
1941	33.5	12.5
1942	−0.9	0.8
1943	53.9	15.6
1944	14.5	5.4
1945	14.6	0.8
Average Return	13.2	−0.5
Standard Deviation	29.2	12.4
Minimum	−40.1	−25.0
Maximum	56.0	21.5

achieved an average annual return of 13.2 percent compared to the U.K. market return, which remained basically flat. Considering that the time period included both the Great Depression and World War II, we would have to say that Keynes's performance was extraordinary.

Even so, the Chest Fund endured some painful periods. In three separate years (1930, 1938, and 1940), its value dropped significantly more than the overall U.K. market. "From the large swings in the Fund's fortune, it is obvious that the Fund must have been more volatile than the market."[5] Indeed, if we measure the standard deviation of the Chest Fund, we find it was almost two and a half times more volatile than the general market. Without a doubt, investors in the Fund received a "bumpy ride" but, in the end, outscored the market by a significantly large margin.

Lest you think Keynes, with his macroeconomic background, possessed market timing skills, take further note of his investment policy.

"We have not proved able to take much advantage of a general systematic movement out of and into ordinary shares as a whole at different phases of the trade cycle. As a result of these experiences I am clear that the idea of wholesale shifts is for various reasons impracticable and indeed undesirable. Most of those who attempt to sell too late and buy too late, and do both too often, incurring heavy expenses and developing too unsettled and speculative a state of mind, which, if it is widespread has besides the grave social disadvantage of aggravating the scale of the fluctuations."[6]

BUFFETT PARTNERSHIP, LTD.

When Warren Buffett returned to Omaha in 1956 after Ben Graham dissolved his investment company, he began the limited investment partnership that we met in Chapter 2. At its opening, the partnership had a total funding of $105,100—a combined contribution of $105,000 from the seven limited partners, and $100 from Buffett. He set himself a tough goal: to beat the Dow Jones Industrial Average by ten points each year. He achieved that and much more. For the thirteen years of the partnership's existence, its average annual return was 22 percent higher than the Dow. In all that time, he never had a down year. By 1965, the partnership's assets were $26 million.

The Buffett Partnership operated between 1957 and 1969, and its returns (see Table 3.2) were both remarkable and somewhat abnormal. Remarkable in that Buffett creamed the Dow's average annual return by twenty-two percentage points over the period, and abnormal in that he was able to achieve the return with less volatility. Note in Table 3.2 that his standard deviation, which is another way to express volatility, is lower than the

Table 3.2   Buffett Partnership, Ltd.

| | Annual Percentage Change | |
| | Overall | Dow Jones |
Year	Partnership (%)	Industrial Average (%)
1957	10.4	−8.4
1958	40.9	38.5
1959	25.9	20.0
1960	22.8	−6.2
1961	45.9	22.4
1962	13.9	−7.6
1963	38.7	20.6
1964	27.8	18.7
1965	47.2	14.2
1966	20.4	−15.6
1967	35.9	19.0
1968	58.8	7.7
1969	6.8	−11.6
Average Return	30.4	8.6
Standard Deviation	15.7	16.7
Minimum	6.8	−15.6
Maximum	58.8	38.5

Dow's. In his typical self-effacing way, Buffett quietly remarked, "I think that any way you figure it, it has been satisfactory."[7]

How did he do it? How did he manage to avoid the volatility that is usually associated with focused portfolios? Two possible explanations come to mind. First, he could have owned securities whose prices moved in dissimilar fashion. Although I am sure he did not purposely construct a low-covariance portfolio, a portfolio that was carefully designed to be economically diverse would likely smooth the bumps in the road. Another possible explanation, which is far more likely, is that Buffett's careful and disciplined approach to purchasing only securities that demonstrated a significant discount to their intrinsic value worked to limit his downside price risk while giving the partnership all the upside benefits.

CHARLES MUNGER PARTNERSHIP

Warren Buffett is often called the world's greatest investor, and that title is richly deserved. However, the outstanding record that Berkshire Hathaway has earned over the years comes not only from Buffett but from the wise counsel of Vice Chairman Charles Munger. The one regret I have about *The Warren Buffett Way* was underserving the important role Charlie has had in Buffett's thinking and Berkshire's fortune. Although Berkshire's investment performance is assigned to its chairman, we should never forget that Charlie is an outstanding investor himself. Shareholders who have attended Berkshire's annual meeting or read Charlie's thoughts in *Outstanding Investor Digest* realize what a fine intellect he has.

"I ran into him in about 1960," said Buffett, "and I told him law was fine as a hobby but he could better."[8] Charlie was a

Harvard Law graduate and, at the time, had a thriving practice in Los Angeles. However, Buffett convinced Charlie to take up investing, and the results of his talents can be found in Table 3.3. "His portfolio was concentrated in very few securities and therefore, his record was much more volatile," explained Buffett, "but it was based on the same discount-from-value approach." Charlie followed the Graham methodology and would look only at companies that were selling below their intrinsic value. "He was willing to accept greater peaks and valleys in performance, and he happens to be a fellow whose psyche goes toward concentration."

Table 3.3 Charles Munger Partnership

| | Annual Percentage Change | |
| | Overall | Dow Jones |
Year	Partnership (%)	Industrial Average (%)
1962	30.1	−7.6
1963	71.7	20.6
1964	49.7	18.7
1965	8.4	14.2
1966	12.4	−15.8
1967	56.2	19.0
1968	40.4	7.7
1969	28.3	−11.6
1970	−0.1	8.7
1971	25.4	9.8
1972	8.3	18.2
1973	−31.9	−13.1
1974	−31.5	−23.1
1975	73.2	44.4
Average Return	24.3	6.4
Standard Deviation	33.0	18.5
Minimum	−31.9	−23.1
Maximum	73.2	44.4

Notice that Buffett does not use the word *risk* in describing Charlie's performance. Using the conventional definition of risk (price volatility), we would have to say that Charlie's partnership was extremely risky, with a standard deviation almost twice that of the market. But beating the average annual return of the market by eighteen points was the act not of a risky man, but rather of an astute investor who was able to focus on a few outstanding stocks that were selling well below their calculated value.

SEQUOIA FUND

Buffett first met Bill Ruane in 1951, when both were taking Ben Graham's security analysis class at Columbia. The two classmates stayed in contact, and Buffett watched Ruane's investment performance over the years with admiration. When Buffett closed his investment partnership in 1969, he got in touch with Ruane. "I asked Bill if he would set up a fund to handle all of our partners, so he set up the Sequoia Fund."

Both men knew it was a difficult time to start a mutual fund, but Ruane plunged ahead. The stock market was splitting into a two-tier market. Most of the hot money was gyrating toward the Nifty Fifty (the big-name companies like IBM and Xerox), leaving the "value" stocks far behind. Although, as Buffett pointed out, comparative performance for value investors was difficult in the beginning, "I am happy to say that my partners, to an amazing degree, not only stayed with him but added money, with happy results."[9]

Sequoia Fund was a true pioneer, the first mutual fund run on the principles of focus investing. We have the public record of Sequoia's holdings, and it demonstrates clearly that Bill Ruane and his partner Rick Cuniff managed a tightly focused low-turnover portfolio. On average, Sequoia owned between six and ten companies that represented well over 90 percent of the portfolio. Even so, the economic diversity of the portfolio was, and continues to be, broad. Ruane has often pointed out that even though Sequoia is a focused portfolio, it has owned a variety of businesses, including commercial banks, pharmaceuticals, and automobile and property casualty insurance.

Bill Ruane's point of view is, in many ways, unique among mutual fund managers. Generally speaking, most investment management begins with some preconceived notion about portfolio management and then fills in the portfolio with various stocks. At Ruane, Cuniff & Company, they begin with the idea of selecting the best possible stocks and then let the portfolio form around those selections.

Selecting the best possible stocks, of course, requires a high level of research; here again, Ruane, Cuniff & Company stands apart from the rest of the industry. The firm has built a reputation as one of the brightest shops in money management. It eschews Wall Street's broker-fed research reports and, instead, relies on its own intensive company investigations. "We don't go in much for titles at our firm," Ruane once said, "[but] if we did, my business card would read 'Bill Ruane, Research Analyst.'"

Such thinking is unusual on Wall Street, he explains. "Typically, people start out their careers in an 'analyst' function but aspire to get promoted to the more prestigious 'portfolio manager' designation, which is considered to be a distinct and higher function. To the contrary, we have always believed that if you are a long-term investor, the analyst function is paramount and the portfolio management follows naturally."[10]

How well has this unique approach served the firm's shareholders? Table 3.4 outlines the investment performance of Sequoia Fund from 1971 through 1997. During this period, Sequoia earned an average annual return of 19.6 percent compared to the

Table 3.4   Sequoia Fund, Inc.

Year	Annual Percentage Change	
	Sequoia Fund (%)	S&P 500 (%)
1971	13.5	14.3
1972	3.7	18.9
1973	−24.0	−14.8
1974	−15.7	−26.4
1975	60.5	37.2
1976	72.3	23.6
1977	19.9	−7.4
1978	23.9	6.4
1979	12.1	18.2
1980	12.6	32.3
1981	21.5	-5.0
1982	31.2	21.4
1983	27.3	22.4
1984	18.5	6.1
1985	28.0	31.6
1986	13.3	18.6
1987	7.4	5.2
1988	11.1	16.5
1989	27.9	31.6
1990	−3.8	−3.1
1991	40.0	30.3
1992	9.4	7.6
1993	10.8	10.0
1994	3.3	1.4
1995	41.4	37.5
1996	21.7	22.9
1997	42.3	33.4
Average Return	19.6	14.5
Standard Deviation	20.6	16.4
Minimum	−24.0	−26.4
Maximum	72.3	37.5

14.5 percent of the S&P 500. Like other focus portfolios, Sequoia achieved this above-average return with a slightly bumpier ride. During this period, the standard deviation of the market (which, you remember, is one way to express volatility) was 16.4 percent compared to Sequoia's 20.6 percent. Some might call that a higher risk, but given the care and diligence of Ruane, Cuniff & Company in selecting stocks, the conventional definition of risk does not apply here.

LOU SIMPSON

At the beginning of 1996, Berkshire Hathaway completed the purchase of GEICO, Inc.—at that time, the seventh largest automobile insurer in the country. It was the culmination of a long and profitable relationship.

Among those who have followed Warren Buffett over the years, GEICO is a familiar name. The company holds a revered place in Berkshire Hathaway. Buffett was introduced to GEICO in 1951 by his teacher, Ben Graham, who was then a director of the company. In true Buffett fashion, Warren traveled to GEICO's headquarters one cold Saturday morning in January to learn more about the business. Lorimer Davidson, who was then assistant to the president and later became CEO, gave Buffett a quick education about GEICO's competitive advantage.

When he returned to Omaha to work at his father's brokerage firm, Buffett focused his efforts on buying shares of GEICO for his clients. He even wrote a research report about GEICO in *The Commercial and Financial Chronicle* titled "The Security I Like Best." By year-end 1951, young Buffett had 65 percent of his net worth—$10,000—invested in GEICO.

In the early 1970s, GEICO ran into problems. Several years of underpricing its policies had produced losses that almost bankrupted the company. Buffett, however, applying his own tenets, was undeterred. He was confident that he was looking at a solid company experiencing temporary difficulties that made its stock price a bargain, and he began acquiring shares. By 1980, through Berkshire Hathaway, he had accumulated 33 percent of GEICO for $45.7 million.

About that same time, Buffett made another acquisition that would have a direct benefit on the financial health of GEICO. His name was Lou Simpson.

Simpson, who had earned a master's degree in economics from Princeton, worked for both Stein Roe & Farnham and Western Asset Management before Buffett lured him to GEICO in 1979. Recalling Simpson's job interview, Buffett remembers that Lou had "the ideal temperament for investing."[11] According to Buffett, Lou was an independent thinker who was confident of his own research and "who derived no particular pleasure from operating with or against the crowd."

Lou is a voracious reader who ignores Wall Street research and instead pores over annual reports. His common-stock selection process is similar to Buffett's. He purchases only high-return businesses that are run by able management and are available at reasonable prices. Lou has something else in common with Buffett. He focuses his portfolio on only a few stocks. GEICO's billion-dollar equity portfolio customarily owns fewer than ten stocks.

Between 1980 and 1996, the equity returns in GEICO's portfolio achieved an average annual return of 24.7 percent compared to the market's return of 17.8 percent (see Table 3.5). "These are not only terrific figures," says Buffett, "but, fully as important, they have been achieved in the right way. Lou has

Table 3.5 Lou Simpson, GEICO

| Year | Annual Percentage Change | |
	GEICO Equities (%)	S&P 500 (%)
1980	23.7	32.3
1981	5.4	−5.0
1982	45.8	21.4
1983	36.0	22.4
1984	21.8	6.1
1985	45.8	31.6
1986	38.7	18.6
1987	−10.0	5.1
1988	30.0	16.6
1989	36.1	31.7
1990	−9.1	−3.1
1991	57.1	30.5
1992	10.7	7.6
1993	5.1	10.1
1994	13.3	1.3
1995	39.7	37.6
1996	29.2	37.6
Average Return	24.7	17.8
Standard Deviation	19.5	14.3
Minimum	−10.0	−5.0
Maximum	57.1	37.6

consistently invested in undervalued common stocks that, individually, were unlikely to present him with a permanent loss and that, collectively, were close to risk-free."[12] Once again, in Buffett's mind, the estimate of risk has nothing to do with volatility. It is based on the certainty that the individual stocks will, over time, produce a profit.

Simpson's performance and investment style fit neatly with Buffett's way of thinking. "Lou takes the same conservative concentrated approach to investments that we do at Berkshire, and it is an enormous plus for us to have him on board," says Buffett.[13] Buffett's admiration for Simpson is great. "There are very few people who I will let run money and businesses that we have control over, but we are delighted in the case of Lou."[14] "His presence on the scene assures us that Berkshire would have an extraordinary professional immediately available to handle its investments if something were to happen to Charlie and me."[15]

Keynes, Buffett, Munger, Ruane, Simpson. It is clear that the Superinvestors of Buffettville have a common intellectual approach to investing. They are united in their belief that the way to reduce risk is to buy stocks only when the margin of safety (that is, the favorable discrepancy between the intrinsic value of the company and today's market price) is high. They also believe that concentrating their portfolio around a limited number of these high-probability events not only reduces risk, but helps to generate returns far above the market rate of return.

Still, when we point out these successful focus investors, many people remain skeptical: perhaps the success is based on their close professional relationship. But all these stock pickers picked different stocks. Buffett didn't own what Munger owned, and Munger didn't own what Ruane owned; Ruane didn't own what Simpson owned, and nobody owned what Keynes owned.

Well, that may be true, say the skeptics, but you've only shown us five examples of focus investors. Five observations are not enough to draw a statistically meaningful conclusion. In an industry that has thousands of portfolio managers, five successes could simply be random chance.

Fair enough. To eliminate any notion that the five Superinvestors of Buffettville are nothing more than statistical aberrations, we need to examine a wider field. Unfortunately, we do not have a large number of focus investors to study, so how do we proceed? By going inside a statistical laboratory and designing a universe of 12,000 portfolios.

THREE THOUSAND FOCUS INVESTORS

Using the Compustat database of common stock returns, we isolated 1,200 companies that displayed measurable data, including revenues, earnings, and return on equity, from 1979 through 1986.[16] We then asked the computer to randomly assemble, from these 1,200 companies, 12,000 portfolios of various sizes:

1. 3,000 portfolios containing 250 stocks.
2. 3,000 portfolios containing 100 stocks.
3. 3,000 portfolios containing 50 stocks.
4. 3,000 portfolios containing 15 stocks.

Next, we calculated the average annual rate of return of each portfolio in each group over two time periods—ten years and eighteen years—and plotted the distribution of these returns as shown in Figures 3.1 and 3.2, respectively. Then, we compared the returns of the four portfolio groups to the overall stock market, defined as the Standard & Poor's 500 Price Index (S&P 500) for the same time periods. From all this, one key finding emerged: In every case, when we reduced the number of stocks in a portfolio, we began to increase the probability of generating returns that were higher than the market's rate of return.

Let's look a little deeper, starting with the ten-year time frame (Figure 3.1). All four portfolio groups had an average yearly return of around 13.8 percent; the S&P 500 average for the same period was somewhat higher: 15.2 percent. Keep two important points in mind: the S&P 500 is a weighted index dominated by the

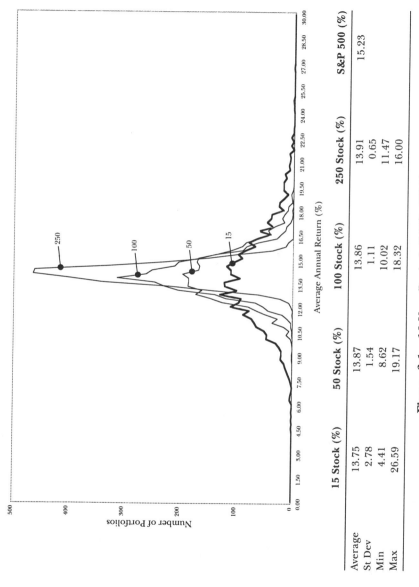

	15 Stock (%)	50 Stock (%)	100 Stock (%)	250 Stock (%)	S&P 500 (%)
Average	13.75	13.87	13.86	13.91	15.23
St Dev	2.78	1.54	1.11	0.65	
Min	4.41	8.62	10.02	11.47	
Max	26.59	19.17	18.32	16.00	

Figure 3.1 10-Year Period (1987–1996).

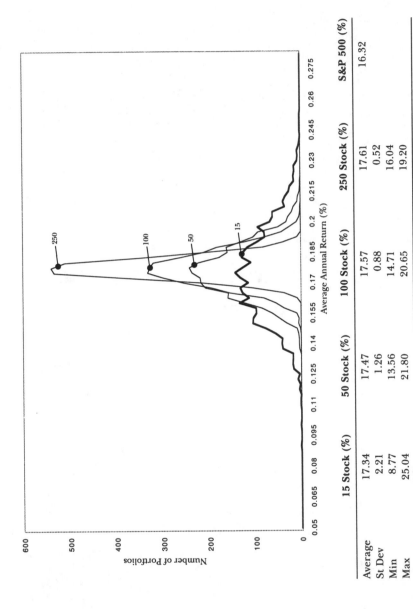

	15 Stock (%)	50 Stock (%)	100 Stock (%)	250 Stock (%)	S&P 500 (%)
Average	17.34	17.47	17.57	17.61	16.32
St Dev	2.21	1.26	0.88	0.52	
Min	8.77	13.56	14.71	16.04	
Max	25.04	21.80	20.65	19.20	

Figure 3.2 18-Year Period (1979–1996).

largest companies, and the time period under consideration was one in which large-capitalization stocks did particularly well. In our study, the portfolios were equally weighted, and they included not only large capitalization stocks but small and midsize companies as well. So we can say that the four groups of "laboratory" portfolios performed approximately on a par with the general market.

This exercise starts to get more interesting when we look at the minimum/maximum numbers—the worst performing and best performing portfolios in each group. Here's what we find:

1. Among the 250-stock portfolios, the best return was 16.0 percent and the worst was 11.4 percent.
2. Among the 100-stock portfolios, the best return was 18.3 percent and the worst was 10.0 percent.
3. Among the 50-stock portfolios, the best return was 19.1 percent and the worst was 8.6 percent.
4. Among the 15-stock portfolios, the best return was 26.6 percent and the worst was 4.4 percent. These were the focus portfolios in the study, and only in this group were the best returns substantially higher than the S&P 500.

The same relative trends were found in the longer (eighteen-year) period (Figure 3.2). The small portfolios showed much higher highs and lower lows than the large portfolios. These results lead us to two inescapable conclusions:

1. You have a much higher chance of doing better than the market with a focus portfolio.
2. You also have a much higher chance of doing worse than the market with a focus portfolio.

To reinforce the first conclusion for the skeptics, we found some remarkable statistics when we sorted the ten-year data:

- Out of 3,000 15-stock portfolios, 808 beat the market.
- Out of 3,000 50-stock portfolios, 549 beat the market.
- Out of 3,000 100-stock portfolios, 337 beat the market.
- Out of 3,000 250-stock portfolios, 63 beat the market.

I submit this as convincing evidence that the probabilities go up as the size of the portfolio goes down. With a 15-stock portfolio, you have a 1-in-4 chance of outperforming the market. With a 250-stock portfolio, your chances are 1 in 50.[17]

Another important consideration: in our study, we did not factor in the effect of trading expenses; obviously, where the turnover rate is higher, so are the costs. If these realized expenses had been included in our graphs, the annualized returns would have shifted to the left, making it even harder to beat a market rate of return.

The second conclusion simply reinforces the critical importance of intelligent stock selection. It is no coincidence that the Superinvestors of Buffettville have also been superior stock pickers. If you have not picked the right companies your underperformance will be striking. However, we can suggest that the outsized returns earned by the Superinvestors have been made possible by their willingness to focus their portfolios on their best ideas—a point that becomes crystal clear when we analyze the common stock portfolio of Berkshire Hathaway.

BERKSHIRE HATHAWAY

Over the past thirty-three years (1965–1997), the per-share book value of Berkshire Hathaway has grown at an average annual rate of 24.9 percent—almost twice the rate of the S&P 500 (see Table 3.6). At this rate, the per-share book value of

Table 3.6 Berkshire Hathaway Inc.

| Year | Annual Percentage Change | |
	Per-Share Book Value of Berkshire (%)	S&P 500 (%)
1965	23.8	10.0
1966	20.3	−11.7
1967	11.0	30.9
1968	19.0	11.0
1969	16.2	−8.4
1970	12.0	3.9
1971	16.4	14.6
1972	21.7	18.9
1973	4.7	−14.8
1974	5.5	−26.4
1975	21.9	37.2
1976	59.3	23.6
1977	31.9	−7.4
1978	24.0	6.4
1979	35.7	18.2
1980	19.3	32.3
1981	31.4	−5.0
1982	40.0	21.4
1983	32.3	22.4
1984	13.6	6.1
1985	48.2	31.6
1986	26.1	18.6
1987	19.5	5.1
1988	20.1	16.6
1989	44.4	31.7
1990	7.4	−3.1
1991	39.6	30.5
1992	20.3	7.6
1993	14.3	10.1
1994	13.9	1.3
1995	43.1	37.6
1996	31.8	23.0
1997	34.1	33.4
Average Return	24.9	12.9
Standard Deviation	13.0	16.4
Minimum	4.7	−26.4
Maximum	59.3	37.6

Berkshire has doubled every 2.9 years. Now you know why there are so many Berkshire Hathaway millionaires. They've been compounding at an above-average rate for thirty years.

Book value is a good measure for judging the company's progress over time, but it muddies our analysis of portfolio management. Berkshire's book value includes not only its common stock holdings but also its fixed-income investments and its closely held businesses. Lumped into Berkshire's book value performance record is the book value of See's Candy Shops, Nebraska Furniture Mart, Buffalo News, Flight Safety, and Scott Fetzer. What would we find if we stripped away all of the non-common-stock investments and analyzed Berkshire's equity portfolio separately? The results are eye-popping.

For this analysis, we isolated Berkshire's equity portfolio as reported annually from 1988 through 1997 (see Table 3.7). We

Table 3.7   Berkshire Equity Portfolio Annual Report

Year	Equity Portfolio Return (%)	Equally Weighted Return (%)	2% Weighted Return (%)	S&P 500 Return (%)
1988	11.9	11.0	16.0	16.6
1989	53.1	38.3	32.3	31.7
1990	2.7	−9.8	−3.9	−3.1
1991	55.5	52.7	33.5	30.4
1992	24.2	31.1	11.4	7.6
1993	11.7	19.5	11.6	10.1
1994	15.3	8.0	2.6	1.3
1995	43.6	43.2	38.3	37.6
1996	37.5	29.6	24.0	23.0
1997	38.5	46.1	35.4	33.4
Average Annual Return	29.4	27.0	20.1	18.9

limited the study to the company's listed primary holdings and ignored the unidentified group referred to as "Other common stock holdings." Because we cannot identify these holdings and because they represent such a small percentage of the equity portfolio, deleting their returns from the study does not meaningfully change the results. One other small caveat: Berkshire reports common stock holdings as of year-end. For our purposes, we assumed that Berkshire owned these securities identically on January 1. Buffett made purchases throughout the year, so to assume each and every position was a full annual return is not correct. However, many of the positions were fully held throughout the year and because we were analyzing a ten-year period, I believe any discrepancy is not significant.

I was first interested to know the return of Berkshire's primary common portfolio over the past ten years. Table 3.7 shows that the average annual return of this group was 29.4 percent, far superior to the S&P 500, which earned 18.9 percent.

Most people who have followed Warren Buffett's career know he is strong on the Coca-Cola Company. The big bets Buffett placed on Coca-Cola over the years paid off handsomely. In 1988, when Buffett began buying the stock, Coca-Cola represented 20.7 percent of the common stock portion of Berkshire's portfolio. From 1991 through 1997, Coca-Cola's position in the portfolio ranged from 34.2 percent to 43 percent. (See Tables A.1 through A.10, pages 208–217 in Appendix A.) And how well did Coca-Cola perform during the ten years from 1988 through 1997? Almost double the regular market: 34.7 percent average return compared to 18.8 percent. It was highly profitable for Buffett to concentrate his position around Coca-Cola. He made a big bet on a high-probability event.

What would have happened if Buffett had not overweighted his positions but had simply maintained an equal balance in his stocks each and every year? To do so, he would have had to sell off a few shares when a position got too big, to bring it back in line with the others. On an equally weighted basis, Berkshire's portfolio would have returned 27.0 percent, just over two and a half percentage points less than the concentrated portfolio.

To take our analysis one last step, let us assume that, instead of a concentrated portfolio, Buffett ran a more broadly diversified portfolio of fifty names. Let us further assume that each of Berkshire's primary holdings (as listed in Tables A.1 through A.10) represented a 2 percent weighting (suggesting a fifty-stock portfolio) and that the balance of the portfolio generated a market rate of return. Although the balance of this fictitious portfolio would include a group of stocks that, on average, could do no better than the market, they could also do no worse. This fictitious portfolio, made up of Berkshire's actual stocks plus market-return stocks, all equally weighted at 2 percent, would have generated a 20.1 percent average annual return over the period—only 1.2 percent better than the market.

Looking back, we can plainly see that the concentrated focus portfolio delivered the best results. Equally weighting the portfolio still beat the market but narrowed the performance spread by just over three percentage points. Finally, the fictitious fifty-stock portfolio, although slightly outperforming the market on average, had the weakest results, dropping down nine percentage points.

This exercise is meant to illustrate, as did our earlier study on 15-, 50-, 100-, and 250-stock portfolios, that focus portfolios that concentrate on high-probability events give the optimal returns. Conversely, attempts to dilute the portfolio with more names in mindlessly equal installments will likely drive returns closer to a market rate of return. When you adjust these returns by subtracting commissions and expenses, you begin to appreciate how difficult it is to outperform the market with hundreds of stocks that are constantly being bought and sold.

THE FLAT EARTH SOCIETY

In his 1984 speech at Columbia, Warren Buffett made the wry observation that if everyone agreed with him and moved over to the focus style of investing, he would be destroying some of his own advantage because the spread between value and price would shrink. But, he quickly added, experience has shown that's not likely to happen.

"The secret has been out for fifty years, ever since Ben Graham and Dave Dodd wrote *Security Analysis,* yet I have seen no trend toward value investing in the thirty-five years I've practiced it," Buffett said. "There seems to be some perverse human characteristic that likes to make easy things difficult."[18]

He may be right. Fifteen years later, there has been no rush toward focus investing. You will recall that, in order to have enough observations to make a statistically defensible argument, we had to artificially create portfolios in a computer lab.

Perhaps, as Buffett says, we have even "backed away from the teaching of value investing. . . . It's likely to continue that way. Ships will sail around the world but the Flat Earth Society will flourish. There will continue to be wide discrepancies between price and value in the marketplace and those who read their Graham and Dodd will continue to prosper."[19]

FOUR

A Better Way to Measure Performance

When the price of a stock can be influenced by a "herd" on Wall Street with prices set at the margin by the most emotional person, or the greediest person, or the most depressed person, it is hard to argue that the market always prices rationally. In fact, market prices are frequently nonsensical.

—Warren Buffett

IF BUFFETT IS RIGHT—if market prices are frequently non-sensical—then we are foolish indeed to use price as a sole indicator of performance. Yet we do. Our entire industry is price-myopic. If the price of a particular stock is going up, we assume good things are happening; if the price starts to go down, we assume something bad is happening, and we act accordingly. But if prices are not always completely rational, are we being completely rational when we base our actions on their ups and downs?

This conundrum is vastly exacerbated by another foolish habit: evaluating price performance over very short periods of time. Not only are we depending on the wrong thing (price), Buffett would say, we're looking at it too often and we're too quick to jump when we don't like what we see.

This double-barreled foolishness—this price-based, short-term mentality—is a flawed way of thinking, and it shows up at every level in our business. It is what prompts some people to check stock quotes every day and call their broker so often they have the phone number on speed-dial. It is why institutional investors, with responsibility for billions of dollars, are ready to buy or sell at the snap of a finger. It is the reason managers of mutual funds churn the stocks in the fund's portfolio at dizzying rates—they think it is their job to do so.

Amazingly, those same money managers are the first to urge their clients to remain calm when things start to look shaky. They send out reassuring letters lauding the virtue of staying the course. Why don't they practice what they preach?

It is especially easy to observe this contradiction in the handling of mutual funds, because their managers' actions are so thoroughly documented and scrutinized by the financial press. Because so much information is available, and because mutual funds are so familiar and well understood, I believe we can learn a great deal about the folly of a price-based measure by looking at how it works in mutual funds.

THE DOUBLE STANDARD IN MUTUAL FUNDS

Writing in *Fortune* magazine late in 1997, Joseph Nocera pointed out the obvious inconsistencies between what mutual fund managers recommend to their shareholders—"buy and hold"—and what those same managers do with their own portfolios—buy–sell, buy–sell, buy–sell. Reinforcing his personal observations of this double standard, Nocera quoted Morningstar's Don Phillips: "There is a huge disconnect between what the fund industry does and what it tells investors to do."[1]

The obvious question becomes: If investors are counseled to wisely buy and hold, why do managers frenetically buy and sell stocks each year? The answer, says Nocera, "is that the internal dynamics of the fund industry make it almost impossible for fund managers to look beyond [the] short term."[2] Why? Because the business of mutual funds has turned into a senseless short-term game of who has best performance, measured totally by price.

Today, there is substantial pressure on portfolio managers to generate eye-catching short-term performance numbers. These numbers attract a lot of attention. Every three months, leading publications such as the *Wall Street Journal* and *Barron's* publish quarterly performance rankings of mutual funds. The funds that have done best in the past three months move to the top of the list, are praised by financial commentators on television and in newspapers, rush to put out self-congratulatory advertising and promotion, and attract a flurry of new deposits. Investors, who have been waiting to see which fund manager has the "hot hand," pounce on these rankings. Indeed, quarterly performance rankings are increasingly used to separate the gifted managers from the mediocre.

This fixation on short-term price performance, so acutely obvious in mutual funds, is not limited to them; it dominates thinking throughout our industry. We are no longer in an environment where managers are measured over the long term. Even people who function as their own manager, as many of you may do, are infected by the unhealthy nuances of this environment. In many ways, we have become enslaved to a marketing machine that all but guarantees underperformance. Caught in a vicious circle, there appears to be no way out. But, as we have learned, there *is* a way to improve investment performance. The cruel irony is that the strategy most likely to provide above-average returns over time appears incompatible with how we judge performance—a mutual fund manager's or our own.

THE TORTOISE AND THE HARE

In 1986, V. Eugene Shahan, a Columbia University Business School alumnus and portfolio manager at U.S. Trust, wrote a follow-up article to Buffett's "The Superinvestors of Graham-and-Doddsville." In his piece, titled "Are Short-Term Performance and Value Investing Mutually Exclusive?" Shahan took on the same question that we are now asking: How appropriate is it to measure a money manager's skill on the basis of short-term performance?

He noted that, with the exception of Buffett himself, many of the people Buffett described as "Superinvestors"—undeniably skilled, undeniably successful—faced periods of short-term underperformance. In a money-management version of the tortoise and the hare, Shahan commented, "It may be another of life's ironies that investors principally concerned with short-term performance may very well achieve it, but at the expense of long-term results. The outstanding records of the Superinvestors of Graham-and-Doddsville were compiled with apparent indifference to short-term performance."[3] In today's mutual fund performance derby, he pointed out, many of the Superinvestors of Graham-and-Doddsville would have been overlooked.

The same is true of the Superinvestors of Buffettville, those five focus investors we met in Chapter 3. Table 4.1 shows that they

Table 4.1 The Superinvestors of Buffettville

	Number of Years of Performance	Number of Years of Underperformance	Underperformance Years as a Percent of All Years (%)
Keynes	18	6	33
Buffett	13	0	0
Munger	14	5	36
Ruane	27	10	37
Simpson	17	4	24

would have struggled through several difficult periods. Only Buffett, again, went through the performance derby unscathed.

John Maynard Keynes, who managed the Chest Fund for eighteen years, underperformed the market one-third of the time. Indeed, his underperformance of the market during the first three years he managed the Fund put him behind the market by eighteen percentage points (see Table 4.3).

The story is similar at Sequoia Fund. Over the marking period, Sequoia underperformed 37 percent of the time (see Table

Table 4.2 The Superinvestors of Buffettville

	Number of Consecutive Years Underperformed the S&P 500
Keynes	3
Buffett	0
Munger	3
Ruane	4
Simpson	1

Table 4.3 The Superinvestors
of Buffettville

	Worst Relative Performance During the Period of Underperformance (%)
Keynes	−18
Buffett	N/A
Munger	−37
Ruane	−36
Simpson	−15

4.1). Like Keynes, Ruane had difficulty coming of age. "Over the years, we have periodically qualified to be the Kings of Underperformance. We had the blurred vision to start the Sequoia Fund in mid-1970 and suffered the Chinese water-torture of underperforming the S&P four straight years." By the end of 1974, Sequoia was a whopping 36 percentage points behind the market. "We hid under the desk, didn't answer the phones and wondered if the storm would ever clear."[4] The storm did clear. By the end of 1976, Sequoia Fund was 50 percent ahead of the market over the five-and-one-half-year period, and, by 1978, Sequoia had gained 220 percent versus 60 percent for the S&P 500.

Even Charlie Munger couldn't escape the inevitable bumps of focus investing. Over fourteen years, Charlie underperformed 36 percent of the time. Like other focus investors, he had a string of bad luck. From 1972 through 1974, Munger fell behind the market by thirty-seven percentage points. Over seventeen years, Lou Simpson underperformed four years, or 24 percent of the time. His worst relative performance occurred during a one-year period when he was fifteen percentage points behind the market.

Incidentally, we see the same trends when we analyze the behavior of our laboratory focus portfolios. (See Table 4.4.) Of the 3,000 portfolios holding fifteen stocks, 808 beat the market during the ten-year period (1987–1996). Yet of those 808 winners, an astonishing 97 percent endured some period of underperformance—four, five, six, even seven years out of ten.

What do you think would happen to Keynes, Munger, Simpson, and Ruane if they were rookie managers starting their careers in today's environment, in which only the value of one year's performance is considered? They would probably be canned, to their clients' profound loss. Yet, following the argument that the focus strategy does sometimes mean enduring several weak years, we run into a very real problem. How can we tell, using price performance as our sole measure, whether we are looking at a very bright manager who is having a poor year (or

Table 4.4   Focus (15-Stock) Portfolios—10-Year Data (1987–1996)

Number of Years Outperform/Underperform S&P 500	Number of Portfolios	Percentage Total (%)
10—0	0	0.00
9—1	1	0.12
8—2	20	2.48
7—3	128	15.84
6—4	272	33.66
5—5	261	32.30
4—6	105	13.00
3—7	21	2.60
2—8	0	0.00
1—9	0	0.00
0—10	0	0.00

even a poor three years) but will do well over the long haul, or one who is starting a long string of bad years? We can't.

Not that we haven't tried.

Academics and researchers have invested considerable energy trying to determine which money managers, which strategies, have the best chance of beating the market over time. In the past few years, the prestigious *Journal of Finance* has published several articles based on studies by prominent university professors, all asking the same basic question: Is there a pattern to mutual fund performance? Together, these professors have brought considerable intellectual weight and data analysis to the problem, but their findings fail to produce a perfect answer.

Of these studies, four dealt with what academics term "persistence"—the tendency of investors to choose funds with the best recent records because they believe a fund manager's track record is an indication of future performance. This creates a kind of self-fulfilling momentum in which this year's money follows the top fund from the past few years. When this momentum is measured in one-year units (picking next year's winner by buying last year's winner), we describe this as the "hot hands" phenomenon. It is all a matter of trying to predict which funds will do well in the near future by observing what they did in the near past. Can it be done? That was what these studies attempted to find out.

In two separate studies, Mark Carhart of the University of Southern California School of Business Administration and Burton Malkiel of Princeton were unable to find any meaningful correlation between persistence and future performance.[5] In the third study, three professors from the John F. Kennedy School of Government at Harvard (Darryll Hendricks, Jayendu Patel, and Richard Zeckhauser) looked at fifteen years' data and concluded that there appears to be no guarantee that buying this year's "hot hand" manager ensures owning next year's "hot hand" fund.[6] Stephen Brown of the Leonard Stern School of Business at New York University and William Goetzmann from Yale's School of Management concluded that persistence is largely a matter of commonalities in strategy. In other words, among any group of hot hands, we would probably find several managers all following the same strategy.[7]

Working separately, these academics came to the same conclusion: There appears to be no significant evidence available that will help investors locate next year's top performers. Bouncing from one hot fund to the next does nothing to aid investors in building their net worth. Not when "hot" is defined by price performance.

We can well imagine what Warren Buffett might make of these academic studies. For him, the moral of the story is clear: We have to drop our insistence on price as the only measuring stick, and we have to break ourselves of the counterproductive habit of making short-term judgments.

But if price is not the best measuring stick, what are we to use instead? "Nothing" is not a good answer. Even buy-and-hold strategists don't recommend keeping our eyes shut. We have to find another benchmark for measuring performance. Fortunately, there is one, and it is the cornerstone to how Buffett judges his performance and the performance of his operating units at Berkshire Hathaway.

ALTERNATIVE PERFORMANCE BENCHMARKS

Warren Buffett once said he "wouldn't care if the stock market closed for a year or two. After all it closes every Saturday and Sunday and that hasn't bothered me yet."[8] Now it is true that "an active trading market is useful, since it periodically presents us with mouth-watering opportunities," said Buffett. "But by no means is it essential."[9]

To fully appreciate this statement, you need to think carefully about what Buffett said next. "A prolonged suspension of trading in securities we hold would not bother us any more than does the lack of daily quotations for World Book or Fechheimer [two Berkshire Hathaway subsidiaries]. Eventually our economic fate will be determined by the economic fate of the business we own, whether our ownership is partial [in the form of shares of stock] or total."[10]

If you owned a business and there was no daily quote to measure its performance, how would you determine your progress? Likely you would measure the growth in earnings, or perhaps the improvement in operating margins, or a reduction in capital expenditures. You simply would let the economics of the business dictate whether you are increasing or decreasing the value of your business. In Buffett's mind, the litmus test for measuring the performance of a private company is no different than measuring the performance of a publicly traded company.

"Charlie and I let our marketable equities tell us by their operating results—not by their daily, or even yearly, price quotations—whether our investments are successful," explains Buffett. "The market may ignore business success for a while, but it eventually will confirm it."[11]

But can we count on the market to reward us for picking the right economic companies? Can we draw a significantly strong correlation between the operating earnings of a company and its future share price? The answer appears to be "Yes," if we are given the appropriate time horizon.

Using our laboratory group of 1,200 companies, we can readily appreciate the relationship between earnings and share price exhibited over different time periods. (The full details of this correlation are found in Tables B.1 through B.5, in Appendix B, pages 220–221.) In summary, when we set out to determine how closely price and earnings are connected, we learn that the longer the time period, the stronger the correlation:

- With stocks held for three years, the degree of correlation ranged from .131 to .360. (A correlation of .360 means that 36 percent of the variance in price was explained by the variance in earnings.)
- With stocks held for five years, the correlation ranged from .374 to .599.
- In a ten-year holding period, the correlation increased to a range of .593 to .695.
- For the entire eighteen-year period, the correlation between earnings and share price is .688—a significantly meaningful relationship.

This bears out Buffett's thesis that, given enough time, a strong business will eventually command a strong price. He cautions, though, that the translation of earnings into share price is both "uneven" and "unpredictable." Although the relationship between earnings and price strengthens over time, it is not always prescient. "While market values track business values quite well over long periods," Buffett notes, "in any given year the relationship can gyrate capriciously."[12] Sixty-five years ago, Ben Graham gave us the same lesson: "In the short run the market is a voting machine but in the long run it is a weighing machine."[13]

It is clear that Buffett is in no hurry to have the market affirm what he already believes is true. "The speed at which a business's success is recognized, furthermore, is not that important as long as the company's intrinsic value is increasing at a satisfactory rate," he says. "In fact, delayed recognition can be an advantage: It may give us the chance to buy more of a good thing at a bargain price."[14]

LOOK-THROUGH EARNINGS

To help shareholders appreciate the value of Berkshire Hathaway's large common stock investments, Buffett coined the term "look-through" earnings. Berkshire's look-through earnings are made up of the operating earnings of its consolidated businesses (its subsidiaries), the retained earnings of its large common stock investments, and an allowance for the tax that Berkshire would have had to pay if the retained earnings were actually paid out.

Retained earnings are the portion of a company's annual earnings that are not distributed to shareholders in the form of dividends but are reinvested back into the company. Over the years, Berkshire's share of retained earnings from its large common stock holdings, including Coca-Cola, Federal Home Loan Mortgage, Gillette, The Washington Post Company, and others, has been significant; in 1997, the figure was $743 million. Now, under generally accepted accounting principles (GAAP), Berkshire can't report its share of retained earnings in its income statement, even though, as Buffett points out, the retained earnings have obvious value.

The notion of look-through earnings was originally devised for Berkshire's shareholders, but it also represents an important lesson for focus investors who seek a way to understand the value of their portfolio when, as will happen from time to time, share prices disengage from underlying economics. "The goal of each investor," says Buffett, "should be to create a portfolio (in effect, a 'company') that will deliver him or her the highest possible look-through earnings a decade or so from now."[15]

According to Buffett, since 1965 (the year Buffett took control of Berkshire Hathaway), the company's look-through earnings have grown at almost the identical rate of the market value of its securities. However, the two have not always moved in lock-step. There have been many occasions when earnings moved ahead of prices (when Ben Graham's famous Mr. Market was unduly depressed). At other times, prices moved far ahead of earnings (when Mr. Market was uncontrollably enthused). What is important to remember is that the relationship works over time. "An approach of this kind," counsels Buffett, "will force the investor to think about long-term business prospects rather than short-term market prospects, a perspective likely to improve results."[16]

BUFFETT'S MEASURING STICK

When Buffett considers adding an investment, he first looks at what he already owns, to see whether the new purchase is any better. What Berkshire owns today is an economic measuring stick used to compare possible acquisitions. "What Buffett is saying is something very useful to practically any investor," stresses Charlie Munger. "For an ordinary individual, the best thing you already have should be your measuring stick." What happens next is one of the most critical but widely overlooked secrets to increasing the value of your portfolio. "If the new thing [you are considering purchasing] isn't better than what you already know is available," says Charlie, "then it hasn't met your threshold. This screens out 99 percent of what you see." (OID)[17]

You already have at your disposal, with what you now own, an economic benchmark—a measuring stick. You can define your own personal economic benchmark in several different ways: look-through earnings, return on equity, or margin of safety, for example. When you buy or sell a company in your portfolio, you have either raised or lowered your economic benchmark. The job of a portfolio manager, who is a long-term owner of securities and believes future stock prices eventually match with underlying economics—and that manager might well be you—is to find ways to raise the benchmark. "That's an enormous thought-conserver," says Munger, "and it's not taught at the business schools by and large." (OID)[18]

If you step back and think for a moment, the S&P 500 is a measuring stick. It is made up of five hundred companies, and each has its own economic return. To outperform the S&P 500 over time—to raise that benchmark—we have to assemble and manage a portfolio of companies whose economics are superior to the average weighted economics of the index. The process of managing such a portfolio is what this book is all about.

Tom Murphy, who ran Capital Cities/ABC before merging it with The Walt Disney Company, understood economic benchmarks perfectly. Inside Cap Cities was a group of media companies that, on a combined weighted basis, produced an economic return for shareholders. Murphy knew that, to increase the value of Cap Cities, he had to find companies that could raise the existing economic benchmark. "The job of manager," Murphy once said, "is not to find ways to make the train longer but to find ways to make it run faster."[19]

You should not be lulled into thinking that just because a focus portfolio lags the stock market on a price basis from time to time, you are excused from the ongoing responsibility of performance scrutiny. With the advent of economic benchmarks, you will, despite the vagaries of the market, still have to defend your individual picks. Granted, a focus manager should not become a slave to the stock market's whims, but you should always be acutely aware of all economic stirrings of the companies in your portfolio.

After all, if a focus manager hasn't got the economics right in the portfolio, it is unlikely Mr. Market (to whom you will be reintroduced in Chapter 7) will ever find an occasion to reward the selections.

TWO GOOD REASONS
TO MOVE LIKE A SLOTH

Focus investing is necessarily a long-term approach to investing. If we were to ask Buffett what he considers an ideal holding period, he would answer "Forever"—so long as the company continues to generate above-average economics and management allocates the earnings of the company in a rational manner. "Inactivity strikes us as intelligent behavior," he explains. "Neither we nor most business managers would dream of feverishly trading highly profitable subsidiaries because a small move in the Federal Reserve's discount rate was predicted or because some Wall Street pundit has reversed his views on the market. Why, then, should we behave differently with our minority positions in wonderful businesses?"[20]

If you own a lousy company, you require turnover because, without it, you end up owning, for a long term, the economics of a sub-par business. But if you own a superior company, the last thing you want to do is to sell it. "When carried out capably, a [low-turnover] investment strategy will often result in its practitioner owning a few securities that will come to represent a very large portion of his portfolio," explains Buffett. "This investor would get a similar result if he followed a policy of purchasing an interest in, say, 20 percent of the future earnings of a number of outstanding college basketball stars. A handful of these would go on to achieve NBA stardom, and the investor's take from them would soon dominate his royalty stream. To suggest that this investor should sell off portions of his most successful investments simply because they have come to dominate his portfolio is akin to suggesting that the Bulls trade Michael Jordan because he has become so important to the team."[21]

This "sloth-like" approach to portfolio management may appear quirky to those accustomed to actively buying and selling stocks on a regular basis, but it does have two important economic benefits, in addition to growing capital at an above-average rate:

1. It works to reduce transaction costs.
2. It increases after-tax returns.

Each advantage by itself is extremely valuable; their combined benefit is enormous.

Reduced Transaction Costs

On average, mutual funds generate between 100 percent and 200 percent turnover ratios each year. The turnover ratio describes the amount of activity in a portfolio. For example, if a portfolio manager sells and re-buys all the stocks in the portfolio once a year, or half the portfolio twice, the turnover ratio is 100 percent. Sell and re-buy everything twice a year, and you have 200 percent turnover. But if a manager sells and re-buys only 10 percent of the portfolio in a year (implying an average ten-year holding period), the turnover ratio is a lowly 10 percent.

In a review of 3,560 domestic stock funds, Morningstar, the Chicago-based researcher of mutual funds, discovered that funds with low turnover ratios generated superior returns compared to funds with higher turnover ratios. The Morningstar study found that, over a ten-year period, funds with turnover ratios of less than 20 percent were able to achieve returns 14 percent higher than funds with turnover rates of more than 100 percent.[22]

This is one of those "commonsense" dynamics that is so obvious it is easily overlooked. The problem with high turnover is that all that trading adds brokerage costs to the fund, which works to lower your net returns.

After-Tax Returns

Low-turnover funds have another important economic advantage: the positive effect of postponing capital gains tax. Ironically, turnover, which is supposed to increase your returns in a fund, also increases your current tax liability. When a manager sells a stock and replaces it with another stock, the belief is that the move will enhance the fund's return. But selling a stock means that a capital gain is realized, so each new pick has the anchor of outperforming the capital gains tax associated with the stock it replaced.

If you own an Individual Retirement Account or a 401(k) plan, you do not pay taxes on their earnings or gain, but if you own a mutual fund in your personal account, any realized capital gains generated in the fund will be passed down to shareholders, triggering a capital gains tax for you. The more stocks are sold from the fund, the more tax liability you may face.

Even when the year-end performance of a mutual fund shows a competitive return, by the time you have paid the taxes on the gains realized, your net after-tax return may very well be below average. Savvy shareholders are starting to ask whether the return provided by their actively managed fund is high enough to pay the taxes owed and still generate a return higher than index funds, which are, by their nature, very tax-efficient.

Except in the case of nontaxable accounts, taxes are the biggest expense that investors face. They are higher than broker-age commissions and often higher than the expense ratio of run-ning a fund. In fact, taxes have become one of the principal reasons why funds generate poor returns. "That is the bad news," according to money managers Robert Jeffrey and Robert Arnott. They are the authors of "Is Your Alpha Big Enough to Cover Its Taxes?" an article that appeared in the well-respected *Journal of Portfolio Management* and generated extensive discussion in the investment world. "The good news," they write, "is that there are trading strategies that can minimize these typically overlooked tax consequences."[23]

In a nutshell, the key strategy involves another of those com-monsense notions that is often underappreciated: the enormous value of the unrealized gain. When a stock appreciates in price *but is not sold,* the increase in value is unrealized gain. No capital gains tax is owed until the stock is sold. If you leave the gain in place, your money compounds more forcefully.

Overall, investors have too often underestimated the enor-mous value of this unrealized gain—what Buffett calls an "inter-est-free loan from the Treasury." To make his point, Buffett asks us to imagine what happens if you buy a $1 investment that dou-bles in price each year. If you sell the investment at the end of the first year, you would have a net gain of $.66 (assuming you're in the 34 percent tax bracket). In the second year, you reinvest $1.66 and it doubles in value by year-end. If the investment con-tinues to double each year, and you continue to sell, pay the tax, and reinvest the proceeds, at the end of twenty years you would have a net gain of $25,200 after paying taxes of $13,000. If, on the other hand, you purchased a $1 investment that doubled each year and was not sold until the *end* of twenty years, you

---

The Amazing Effect of Compounding

Start with a $1 investment that doubles in value every year.

1. Sell the investment at the end of the year, pay the tax, and reinvest the net proceeds.
   Do the same thing every year for twenty years.
   End up with $25,200 clear profit.

   Or

2. Don't sell anything.
   At the end of twenty years, end up with $692,000 after-tax profit.

---

would gain $692,000 after paying taxes of approximately $356,000.

A cold look at the numbers makes a couple of observations clear. You end up with a great deal more profit if you don't take your gain each year but just let the money compound. At the same time, your lump-sum tax bill at the end of twenty years will take your breath away. That may be one reason people seem to instinctively feel it's better to convert the gain each year and thereby keep the taxes under control. What they fail to appreciate is that they are missing out on a truly awesome difference in return.

For their article, Jeffrey and Arnott calculated the point at which turnover begins to negatively impact the portfolio. The answer, surprisingly, is counterintuitive. The greatest tax damage to the portfolio occurs at the outset of turnover and then diminishes as turnover increases. Jeffrey and Arnott write: "Conventional wisdom thinks of any turnover in the range of

1 percent–25 percent as categorically low and inconsequential, and of anything greater than 50 percent as being high and presumably of considerable consequence; the reality is just the opposite."[24]

The Jeffrey–Arnott study shows that, at a 25 percent turnover ratio, the portfolio incurs 80 percent of the taxes that would be generated by a portfolio turnover ratio of 100 percent. They conclude that it is more important to be mindful of turnover ratios in the lower range than in the higher range. To achieve high after-tax returns, investors need to keep their average annual portfolio turnover ratio somewhere between zero and 20 percent.

What strategies lend themselves best to low turnover rates? One possible approach is a passive, low-turnover index fund. Another is a focus portfolio. "It sounds like premarital counseling advice," say Jeffrey and Arnott, "namely, to try to build a portfolio that you can live with for a long, long time."[25]

"In investment management today," explains Charlie Munger, "everybody wants to not only win, but to have a yearly outcome path that never diverges very much from a standard path except on the upside." Well, says Charlie, "from the viewpoint of a rational consumer, the whole system is bonkers and it draws a lot of talented people into socially useless activity." (OID)[26] Portfolio managers counter with: "We have to behave that way. It's how we are measured."

Today, portfolio managers are constrained by relative performance. "In the relative performance game," explains business writer Peter Bernstein, "the risk in your portfolio is no longer in the securities you own. The greater risk is in the far larger number of stocks you don't own. You're short all of them."[27] Portfolio managers run the risk of losing clients and offending consultants if their performance deviates too far from the market return. The fear of "tracking error"—performance that is too far away from the market's return—has, according to Charlie Munger, "hobbled the industry."

We have spent a good deal of this chapter on the ups and downs of mutual funds. We did so, you will recall, because mutual funds are familiar and therefore an easy example. But do not imagine for one minute that the erroneous thinking is limited to managers of mutual funds. They are cited here merely to exemplify the broad trends that thread their way through the entire investment world. By observing what these mutual fund managers do and how they think, we can learn much about what *you* should do and how *you* should think.

What we have learned is that strong short-term performance does not necessarily identify superior portfolio managers any more than weak short-term performance excludes them. The time horizon we use to measure ability is simply too short to draw any meaningful conclusions. However, using alternative economic benchmarks such as look-through earnings may be a way for you to gauge your progress when price deviates from expected returns. We also learned that low turnover translates into higher returns in two simple, obvious ways. Fewer transactions mean lower trading costs. Finally, don't overlook the value of unrealized capital gains. With the exception of passive index funds, focus investing gives you the best opportunity to compound this unrealized gain into major profits.

"The Berkshire system is not bonkers," Charlie Munger concludes. "I'd say that Berkshire Hathaway is adapting to the nature of the investment problem as it really is." (OID)[28]

FIVE

The
Warren Buffett Way
Tool Belt

The investor of today does not profit from yesterday's growth.

—Warren Buffett

WITH *THE WARREN BUFFETT WAY*, I hoped to describe and codify Warren Buffett's style of investing, so that others might benefit from understanding his approach. In that earlier book I outlined the fundamental investment tools, or tenets, by which Buffett evaluates possible purchases. These tenets are summarized in Chapter 1, page 8.

The underlying principles haven't changed much since *The Warren Buffett Way* was published, in 1994 ("That's why they call them principles," Buffett once said), but many readers have asked for clarification about applying the tenets in today's market. Also, the continuing debate about growth versus value deserves our attention, and some newer issues have presented themselves: the economic value added (EVA) approach and the role of technology. Can we use the Warren Buffett Way template to pick technology companies?

MARKET TENET: HOW TO VALUE A BUSINESS

Determining the intrinsic value of a company—the first and most critical step in the Buffett decision process—is both art and science. The science involves a fairly straightforward bit of mathematics.

To calculate the current value of a business, you start by estimating the cash flows that you expect will occur over the life of the business and then discount that total backward to today, using an appropriate discount rate. "If we could see, in looking at any business, its future cash inflows and outflows between the business and its owner over the next 100 years, or until the business is extinct, and then could discount them back at the appropriate interest rate, that would give us a number for intrinsic value," says Buffett. (OID)[1] This concept, postulated by John Burr Williams in *The Theory of Investment Value,* is as true today as it was when first written more than sixty years ago.

Some people find it easier to compare this process to the one used when valuing a bond. The mathematics are the same. Instead of cash flow, bonds have coupons; instead of an indefinite period, bonds have a finite life, at which point they return the invested capital back to the owners. "It would be like looking at a bond with a whole bunch of coupons on it that matured in a hundred years," explains Buffett. "Well, businesses have coupons that are going to develop into the future, too. The only problem is that they aren't printed on the instrument. Therefore, it's up to the investor to estimate what those coupons are going to be." (OID)[2]

Estimating the amount of the coupons, then, is a matter of two numbers: the probable future earnings, and the discount rate used to bring those future earnings back to present dollars. For the second number, the discount rate, Buffett generally uses the rate then current for long-term government bonds. Because the certainty that the U.S. Government will pay its coupon over the next thirty years is virtually 100 percent, we can say that this is a risk-free rate. As Buffett explains, "We use the risk-free rate merely to equate one item to another." (OID)[3] According to Buffett, it is simply the most appropriate yardstick with which to measure a basket of all different investment types: government bonds, corporate bonds, common stocks, apartment buildings, oil wells, and farms.

Buffett does not adjust the discount rate for uncertainty. If one investment appears riskier than another, he keeps the discount rate constant and, instead, adjusts the purchase price. He would, in other words, obtain his margin of safety not by including a premium for "equity risk," as the Capital Asset Pricing Model (CAPM) requires, but by buying at a lower purchase price to begin with. "If you understand a business and if you can see its future perfectly, then you obviously need very little in the way of margin of safety," says Buffett. "Conversely, the more vulnerable the business, the larger the margin of safety you require." (OID)[4]

In *The Warren Buffett Way*, we aligned Buffett's tenets with several of Berkshire Hathaway's largest common stock holdings to create case studies that we could learn from. Several of these case studies involved companies whose "coupons" could reasonably be expected to grow in perpetuity and whose growth in earnings exceeded the risk-free rate. With them, it was necessary to use a two-stage dividend discount model—one growth rate for an initial period, then a lower rate for a second, longer period.

Buffett's 1988 purchase of Coca-Cola is a good example. At the time, the long-term government bond rate was 9 percent and Coca-Cola's growth rate was 15 percent. Subtracting 15 percent from 9 percent would give us a negative number, making the calculation nonsensical. To overcome this limitation, I used the two-stage discount model. First, I started with the assumption that Coca-Cola would grow its owner-earnings (net income plus depreciation/amortization minus capital expenditures) at an above-average rate for at least ten years, then would slow to a more average 5 percent rate thereafter. In year eleven, I then could subtract the 5 percent earnings growth from the 9 percent risk-free rate and get a rate of 4 percent for discounting the company's earnings into the future.

Many of the questions I have been asked since *The Warren Buffett Way* was published have involved the dividend discount model—and specifically, my assumptions. Some readers have argued that Coca-Cola will surely grow its earnings at a 15 percent rate far past ten years, and thus I was too conservative in my projections. Others have insisted that, because looking ahead ten years is far too difficult, I should have used the 15 percent growth rate for only five years.

Both points are valid; hence, neither answer is perfect. But remember what Buffett says: "It is better to be approximately right than precisely wrong." The issue is not so much whether Coca-Cola will grow its cash at a 15 percent rate for five years, seven years, or ten years. The real issue is the need to take the time to do the research and calculate intrinsic value, rather than relying on shortcut methods (such as price–earnings ratio, price-to-book ratio, or relative measures to the market). Although precise to the decimal, these methods tell nothing about the value of an investment.

The other question I am commonly asked in regard to the dividend discount model is: That was all well and good when the risk-free rate was 9 percent, but now it's more like 5 percent or 6 percent. Now what? When the interest rate is 6 percent, using a 5 percent residual growth rate discounts owner earnings at a paltry 1 percent. What would Buffett do?

Buffett tells us that, in a low-interest-rate environment, he adjusts the discount rate upward. When bond yields dipped below 7 percent, Buffett adjusted his discount rate up to 10 percent. If interest rates work themselves higher over time, he has successfully matched his discount rate to the long-term rate. If they do not, he has increased his margin of safety by three additional points.

FINANCIAL TENET: TO EVA OR NOT TO EVA? THAT IS THE QUESTION

There has been little debate about the financial tenets outlined in *The Warren Buffett Way.* No one disagrees that an attractive company is one that enjoys high profit margins and generates cash earnings for its owners. The attraction continues if the net profits of the company earn a high return on the company's equity. However, there has been considerable debate about the economic value added (EVA) approach and whether it has a place in Buffett's thinking.

EVA, trademarked by the New York consulting firm Stern Stewart, is a measurement system that determines whether the return on investment exceeds the cost of capital. Over the past several years, many companies, including Coca-Cola, Eli Lilly, and AT&T, have adopted the EVA approach.

To calculate, start by determining a company's cost of capital; then subtract the company's net earnings. Cost of capital is cost of debt plus cost of equity, in proportionate measures. Cost of debt is simply the interest rate the company pays on borrowed money, adjusted for interest expense deductibility. The cost of equity is determined by the riskiness of the business, as measured by the CAPM.

The weighted average cost of capital, then, is:

Equity percentage of the capital structure × its cost
+ debt percentage × its cost

For example, if a company's capital structure was 60 percent equity and 40 percent debt, and if the equity cost was 15 percent and the interest rate on the debt was 9 percent, the company's weighted average cost of capital would be:

$$60 \text{ percent} \times 15 \text{ percent} + 40 \text{ percent} \times 9 \text{ percent}$$
$$= 12.6 \text{ percent.}$$

If the company went on to earn 15 percent return on capital that cost it 12.6 percent, we can say the company added economic value. If it earns at this higher rate consistently, its share price usually rises. On the other hand, if the company earned 10 percent on its capital for several years running, its share price would typically decline.

EVA is one type of measuring stick, one specific hurdle rate. Buffett has a different measuring stick. He measures a company's hurdle rate by its ability to grow its market value by a rate that is at least equal to the value of the company's retained earnings. For every dollar a company retains, Buffett argues, it should create at least one dollar in market value.

From high above, it may appear that Buffett's one-dollar-retained-for-one-dollar-market value and Stern Stewart's EVA are intellectually similar. But Buffett has trouble embracing the finer points of EVA.

First, the EVA formula is based on the CAPM, which relies on price volatility to measure risk. We already know Buffett's opinion on the idea that a more volatile stock is riskier. Second, because cost of equity is always higher than cost of debt, in the EVA model the cost of capital actually declines when the relative use of debt increases. EVA proponents would have a hard time convincing Buffett, with his liking for companies that are debt-free or close to it, that higher debt is a good thing because it equals lower cost of capital.

The cost of capital is one of the business world's great mysteries. EVA is but one approach that seeks to set that cost. Buffett may not use EVA to calculate the cost of capital, but that doesn't mean he disregards the question. All of Berkshire Hathaway's subsidiaries are charged for the capital they request from Buffett. He acknowledges that he doesn't use complex formulas; rather, "We just figure it's simpler to charge people a fair amount for the money and then let them figure out whether they really want to buy a new splitter or whatever it may be. It varies a little, depending on the history of when we came in and what the interest rate was when we bought it, but generally we charge people something like 15 percent on capital. We find that 15 percent gets their attention, but shouldn't be such a high hurdle rate that things we want to do don't get done." (OID)[5]

It's important to keep in mind that Buffett's internal benchmark for Berkshire Hathaway is that the company overall needs to grow at a minimum rate of 15 percent annually. Therefore, 15 percent is also his hurdle rate for capital. His requirement is that whenever he provides capital to any of the subsidiaries, whatever the capital is used for—a new research facility, new equipment, a new advertising campaign—must ultimately produce a return of at least that same rate.

Berkshire Hathaway and EVA are both setting a cost of capital. Granted, they attack the problem is different ways; but both seek the same end result—to reward companies that earn more than the cost of capital, and to penalize the group that earns less than the cost of capital. As Buffett remarked at Berkshire's 1995 annual meeting, "I don't think it's a very complicated subject. I didn't need [EVA] to know that Coca-Cola has added a lot of value." (OID)[6]

MANAGEMENT TENET:
CAN WE VALUE MANAGERS?

The highest compliment Warren Buffett can pay a manager is to say that the manager unfailingly behaves and thinks like an owner of the company. Managers who behave like owners tend not to lose sight of the company's prime objective—increasing shareholder value—and they tend to make rational decisions that further that goal. But how can we distinguish managers who are actively working to increase shareholder value from their counterparts whose commitment to this idea is only lip service? In other words, can we place a value on management?

Warren Buffett applies three tenets about a company's management: (1) rationality, (2) candor, and (3) resisting the institutional imperative. Because they are described in detail in *The Warren Buffett Way,* these three characteristics are summarized only briefly here.

As we have learned, if a company generates high returns on equity, the duty of management is to reinvest those earnings back into the company, for the benefit of shareholders. However, if the earnings cannot be reinvested at high rates, management has three options: (1) ignore the problem and continue to reinvest at below-average rates; (2) buy growth; or (3) return the money to the shareholders, who then might have a chance to reinvest the money elsewhere at higher rates. In Buffett's mind, only one choice is rational, and that is option 3.

As we attempt to measure the value of management, the decision made at this crossroads gives us a good clue. The choice that management makes will prove either valuable or disappointing for shareholders long before the results are compiled in an annual report.

After rationality, we should look at management's candor. Over time, every company makes mistakes, both large and inconsequential. Too many managers have the tendency to report results with excess optimism rather than honest explanation. There is something admirable about the manager who, with courage, discusses the failures of the company with shareholders. It is Buffett's belief that a manager who confesses mistakes publicly is more likely to correct them.

If allocation of capital is simple and logical, why is capital so poorly allocated? If management stands to gain wisdom and credibility by facing mistakes, why do annual reports trumpet only success? The answer, Buffett has learned, is the unseen force called the *institutional imperative*—the lemming-like tendency of corporate management to imitate the behavior of other managers, no matter how silly or irrational it may be. Thinking independently and charting a course based on rationality and logic are more likely to maximize the profits of the company than a strategy that can best be described as "follow the leader."

Evaluating management along these three dimensions is more difficult than measuring financial performance, for the simple reason that human beings are more complex than numbers. Indeed, many analysts believe that because measuring human activity is vague and imprecise, we cannot value management with any degree of confidence and therefore the exercise is futile. Without a decimal point, they seem to suggest, there is nothing to measure.

Others hold the view that the value of management is fully reflected in the company's performance statistics—including sales, profit margins, and return on equity—and no other measuring stick is necessary.

Both of these opinions have some validity, but neither is, in my view, strong enough to outweigh the original premise. The reason for taking the time to evaluate management is that it gives you early-warning signals of eventual financial performance. If you look closely at the words and actions of a management team, you will find clues for measuring the value of their work long before it shows up in the company's financial reports or in the stock pages of your daily newspaper. Finding the clues will take some digging, and that news may be enough to discourage the weak of heart or the lazy. Their discouragement is your gain.

If the idea of measuring management still seems vague, Buffett offers a few tips:

- Review annual reports from a few years back, paying special attention to what management said then about strategies for the future.
- Compare those plans to today's results: How fully were they realized?
- Compare the strategies of a few years ago to this year's strategies and ideas: How has the thinking changed?
- Compare the annual reports of the company you are interested in with reports from similar companies in the same industry. It is not always easy to find exact duplicates, but even relative performance comparison can yield insights.

A focus investor is ideally suited to the task of measuring management. Someone who owns just a few companies and plans to own them for several years has a real opportunity to get to know management. Track through earlier annual reports and begin to develop a sense of the management's history. Follow your companies in the press; read what management says and what others say about them. If you notice that the CEO recently made a speech or presentation, get a copy from the investor relations department and read it carefully. Search the companies' Web pages for up-to-the-minute information. In every way you can think of, raise your antennae. The important point is: Do not dismiss the premise about valuing management because the task is not simple. The more you keep your eyes open for clues, the more attuned you will be and the easier the process will become.

Perhaps it will help to remember why you are doing all this: You will learn bits of information that will ultimately affect share prices, but you will have them in advance. If, as Buffett suggests, the market is frequently (though not always) efficient, valuing management is the one analytical tool that can put you ahead of the market.

GROWTH VERSUS VALUE: THE CONTINUING DEBATE

Warren Buffett's approach to picking stocks has changed very little over the past twenty years. He thinks about the company, the management, the financials, and the asking price—in that order. It is, by all appearances, a simple, straightforward approach. Yet, for all its simplicity, Buffett's approach to investing is caught in a long-standing intellectual tug-of-war that seeks to distinguish value investing from growth investing.

Traditionally, a "value investor" is someone who is looking for stocks that are selling at a tangible discount to their underlying value—as reflected in a low ratio of price to book value, a low price–earnings ratio, or a high dividend yield. "Growth investors" seek to make money by aligning themselves with companies whose earnings are growing very rapidly and presumably will continue to do so.

"Most analysts," says Buffett, "feel they must choose between two approaches customarily thought to be in opposition: value and growth. Indeed, many investment professionals see any mixing of the two terms as a form of intellectual cross-dressing."[7] Buffett, you may not be surprised to learn, has a different view on "value" and "growth."

The value of a stock, Buffett has explained on several occasions, is the net cash flows of the investment that occur over the life of the investment, discounted at the appropriate interest rate. Growth, he points out, is simply a part of the calculation that pertains to the cash flow. "In our opinion," says Buffett, "the two approaches [value and growth] are joined at the hip."[8]

Charlie Munger, whose few words are always chosen carefully, says: "The whole concept of dividing it up into 'value' and 'growth' strikes me as twaddle. It's convenient for a bunch of pension fund consultants to get fees prattling about and a way for one advisor to distinguish himself from another. But to me, all intelligent investing is value investing." (OID)[9]

Despite Buffett's and Munger's contention that there is no meaningful difference between "growth investing" and "value investing," the investment industry is still obsessed with separating these two functions. If you follow the Warren Buffett Way, you will, from time to time, confront the inevitable question: Are you a growth investor or a value investor? Considering Charlie Munger's point of view, it is probably best to identify yourself as a value investor. But be careful not to fall into the trap of buying stocks simply because they are designated as typical "value" stocks.

One person who has successfully navigated the divide between growth and value is William H. Miller III. Bill's track record is, without question, impressive, but it is how he achieved the investment return that holds a valuable lesson for us all.

BILL MILLER AND
THE LEGG MASON VALUE TRUST

In 1982, Legg Mason, a Baltimore-based brokerage and money management firm, launched its flagship mutual fund, Value

Trust. From 1982 until 1990, Value Trust was comanaged by Ernie Kiehne, the former head of research at Legg Mason, and a bright but untested Bill Miller.

Bill's pathway to the money management business was unusual. While his competitors were tied up in business schools studying modern portfolio theory, Bill was studying philosophy at Johns Hopkins Graduate School. While other money managers-in-training studied Markowitz, Sharpe, and Fama, Bill read William James's *Pragmatism* and John Dewey's *Essays in Experimental Logic*. After a brief period as a corporate treasurer, which helped him understand how companies work, Bill landed at Legg Mason's research department, where he then joined Ernie Kiehne in managing Value Trust.

During the 1980s, Value Trust was an exercise in two disciplines. Ernie followed Ben Graham's approach of buying companies that were selling at low price–earnings ratios and discounts to book value. Bill took a different course. "My approach," he explained, "is more the theoretical approach that Graham talks about and that Warren Buffett has elaborated on, which is that the value of any investment is the present value of the future cash stream. The trick is to value that and thus value the assets rationally and buy them at a big discount."[10]

During 1990, Bill assumed full control of Value Trust and began to put the full weight of his investment approach into the Fund. What happened next was not repeated by any other general equity fund in the 1990s. For eight consecutive years (1991–1998), Value Trust consistently outperformed the S&P 500. At the end of 1998, Bill's outstanding track record brought him one of the industry's most coveted honors: he was named Morningstar's Domestic Equity Fund Manager of the Year.

"Bill takes big positions and takes the long view," said Eric Savitz, formerly of *Barron's*. "Over the long term, you can see how it has worked." Savitz, who followed Bill's success while writing the mutual fund column for *Barron's*, remembers Bill as very low-key. "He was nonpromotional. There were plenty of other money managers who jumped on CNBC and talked themselves up, but Bill is not the kind of person who trumpets his own success. Still, he was more insightful about the stocks than anybody I knew."[11]

Today, Bill manages over $12 billion in assets for Legg Mason, including the $9 billion Value Trust. Although he is not a focus investor by strict definition, he comes very close—he routinely keeps Value Trust in only thirty to forty names, with over half of the assets invested in just ten stocks. "There are several parallels between Bill Miller and Warren Buffett," explains Amy Arnott, editor of *Morningstar*. "He does have a very low turnover strategy and his portfolio is very concentrated compared to other equity funds. His method of valuing companies is similar to Buffett in that they both look at free cash flow as a measure of intrinsic value."[12]

Bill, even though he is a value manager, does not always show up in the "value" area of the style box—the shorthand summary of attributes used by several financial publications. If you look at traditional measures of value, including price to earnings and price to book, Bill does not always fall neatly into this mold. "We're trying to distinguish companies that are deservedly cheap from those that are undeservedly cheap," he explains. "There are a lot of companies that trade at low valuations that are down in price and are not attractive. The trick is to separate the ones that are from those that aren't."[13]

Bill's discriminating taste for companies, coupled with his long holding period, has certainly helped Value Trust achieve its status as one of the best mutual funds of the 1990s, but not without a price. Because Value Trust holds a collection of businesses that appear to be a cross-blend of growth and value companies, Bill has not been able to escape the dogged controversy over whether he is a value manager or a growth manager, as evidenced by Jim Cramer's biting report on *TheStreet.com*.

Cramer, the highly charged and intellectual co-founder of *TheStreet.com*, wrote a scathing piece entitled "Wrong! Rear Echelon Revelations: Mutual Funds and Value Judgements." Cramer openly attacked several value funds that also owned stocks that matched the industry definition of growth stocks. Citing the Value Index chart from *Investor's Business Daily*, Cramer pointed out that several of the value funds in this index also owned large positions in companies that included Dell Computer, America Online, Microsoft, and Lucent. "What a preposterous notion of value these stocks represent. . . . Value. . . . Give me a break," Cramer wrote.

Cramer continued, "I don't want to sound too cynical about this, but I think managers aren't thinking about anything. Mutual funds have about the worst truth-in-labeling problem I have come across in any industry. I think there should be a rule: The term value should not get applied to firms that own such high-multiple stocks. Value in this world has simply become a masquerade, a mean-spirited marketing tactic that lures people in the door who would otherwise have no desire to own such nosebleed stocks."[14]

Miller responded with a letter to *TheStreet.com* that I believe eloquently captures the essence of the growth-versus-value debate. His comments are slightly edited and are reproduced here with permission:

> Jim, Legg Mason Value Trust, the fund I run, may be the offender that set you off in your value/growth column, since we are in the IBD value index, and have Dell and AOL as our largest two positions. (We don't own Lucent or Microsoft.)
>
> Of course, in 1996, when we were buying Dell at $4.00 and trading at 6x with a 40% return on capital, no one thought we were being heretical. And when we were loading up on AOL at $15 in late 1996, people just thought we were nuts to buy something that

was probably going out of business due to either the Internet, or Microsoft, or their own incompetence. [Note that, adjusted for subsequent splits, Bill's purchase of Dell is now $2 per share and AOL is $7.50 per share.]

The issue of course is how can they be value now, with p/e's and p/book in the stratosphere?

Part of the answer has to do with general investment strategy. With money managers turning their portfolios north of 100 percent per year in a frenetic chase to find something that works, our glacial 11% turnover is anomalous. Finding good businesses at cheap prices, taking a big position, and then holding for years used to be sensible investing.

In a speculative market, long-term investing is rare, but it's what we do. We see no reason to sell a good business just because the stock price has gone up a lot, or because some amount of time has passed.

The better answer is that price and value are two different and independent variables. As Buffett has pointed out, there is no theoretical difference between value and growth; the value of any investment is the present value of the future cash flows of the business.

Value and growth do not carve the world at the joints; the terms are mainly used by consultants to allow them to carve the world of money managers up for clients. They represent characteristics of stocks, not of businesses. As Charlie Munger once said, the distinction is "twaddle."

With the market beating 91% of surviving managers since the beginning of 1982, it looks pretty efficient to me. Since a computer is not a scarce resource, and databases are not in short supply, accounting-based stock factors (price/earnings, price/book, price/cash flow, etc.) that the computer can identify and back test are unlikely to lead to robust performance.

Any combination of stock factors that appear to hold the key to outperformance will be quickly arbitraged away. There is no algorithmic way to outperform.

Any portfolio that outperforms over any length of time does so because it contains mispriced securities. The market was wrong about the future of that aggregate. We look directly for mispricings by comparing what the market says a company is worth with what we believe it is worth using a multifactor methodology.

This methodology starts with the accounting-based stuff and moves through private market value analysis, leveraged buyout analysis, looking at liquidating value, and of course involves a discounted cash flow model.

Valuation is a dynamic not a static process. When we first valued AOL it was trading in the mid-teens; we believed the business was worth $30 or so. We now value the business at $110 on the low end to $175, based on what we think is a conservative discounted cash flow. If we are right about the long-term economic model, the number could be much higher.

No one complains when we're loaded with General Motors or Chase—good, old, easy-to-understand values—or when we're buying perpetual dogs like Toys "R" Us or Western Digital in the midst of massive losses. It's the Dells and AOLs people object to.

And what they seem to object to most is that we didn't sell Dell at $8 like other value guys did because historically PC stocks traded between 6 and 12x earnings, so when Dell hit 12x it must no longer be a value.

We are delighted when people use simple-minded, accounting-based metrics and then align them on a linear scale and then use that to make buy-and-sell decisions. It's much easier than actually doing the work to figure out what the business is worth, and it enables us to generate better results for our clients by doing more thorough analysis.

We own GM and AOL for the same reason: The market is wrong about the price because both companies trade at discounts to the intrinsic value of the underlying business.

Best Regards,
Bill Miller

It is a classic argument. I believe Bill's letter will be studied by investors and academicians alike. It certainly caught Jim Cramer's attention. Here is how he responded on *TheStreet.com:*

Dear Bill,

Wow, that was eye-opening. You are truly doing something different. The anomalies of massive price increases, great stock picking by you, and the need to keep taxes low all lead to something special on your part and I certainly apologize that my "value" net piece brought you in. Looks like I have to dig deeper than just a chart with names to understand the "value" conundrum. Excellent work; terrific response and I thank you for taking the time out to share it with us. Oh yes, and congratulations for spotting Dell and AOL so early.

Jim Cramer

In 1998, I joined Bill Miller at Legg Mason, bringing with me the Focus Trust mutual fund and its shareholders. The press took notice of the change and immediately questioned how Focus Trust would fare with a new money management group that widely owned technology companies. "Bill Miller, the world's other great investor, ranks right up there in the pantheon of all-time greats," wrote Sandra Ward at *Barron's*. "Yet, unlike Buffett, Bill Miller's a big believer in technology. Indeed it has been Miller's heavy bets on technology shares, in addition to heavy weightings in financials, that have helped push his performance beyond the benchmarks."[15]

What would happen, these writers were asking, when the Warren Buffett Way blended with the Bill Miller Way? Could we use the Warren Buffett Way to pick technology companies for Focus Trust?

THE WARREN BUFFETT WAY
AND TECHNOLOGY COMPANIES

Because Berkshire Hathaway does not own any technology companies, many people have assumed that technology companies as a group cannot be analyzed with a degree of confidence, or Buffett would have done so.

Not true.

Buffett easily admits that he doesn't feel competent to understand and value technology companies. At the 1998 Berkshire Hathaway annual meeting, he was asked whether he would ever consider investing in the technology group at some point in the future. "Well, the answer is no," he responded, "and it's probably been pretty unfortunate.

"I've been an admirer of Andy Grove and Bill Gates," Buffett continued, "and I wish I'd translated that admiration into action by backing it up with money. But when it comes to Microsoft and Intel, I don't know what the world will look like ten years from now, and I don't want to play in a game where the other guy has an advantage. I could spend all my time thinking about the technology for the next year and still not be the 100th, 1,000th, or even the 10,000th smartest guy in the country in analyzing those businesses. There are people who can analyze technology, but I can't." (OID)[16]

This thinking is echoed by Charlie Munger. "The reason we are not in high-tech businesses is that we have a special lack of aptitude in that area. The advantage of low-tech stuff is that we think we understand it fairly well. The other stuff we don't and we'd rather deal with what we understand. Why should we play a competitive game in a field where we have no advantage—maybe a disadvantage—instead of playing in a field where we have a clear advantage." (OID)[17]

Playing games of only average chance can have a negative impact on one's net worth. Are you willing to bet your life's savings on periodic coin-flipping games? "Each of you will have to figure out where your talents lie," counsels Charlie, "and you will have to use your advantages. But if you try to succeed in what you're worst at, you're going to have a very lousy career. I can almost guarantee it." (OID)[18]

For years, value investors wrongly stayed away from technology companies because of Buffett's lack of activity in this area. Wrongly perceiving that they could not analyze this new industry, they now find themselves far behind the curve among a group of talented competitors.

"Most value investors use historical valuations to determine when stocks are cheap or expensive," explains Bill Miller. "However, if investors use only historical models, their evaluation methodologies become context-dependent." In other words, historical valuation models work as long as the future looks very much like the past. "The problem facing most value investors is that the future is different from the past in many respects," says Miller, "and, importantly, one of the major differences is the role of technology in society.

"Actually, I think that, in many cases, technology lends itself especially well to the Warren Buffett Way template," Miller continues, "which is really just a tool kit for sharpening your analytical ability so you can select, out of the whole universe of potential investments, those that are likely to have the highest probability of giving you an above-average return over a long period."[19]

From that perspective, we can see that several technology companies exhibit the economic traits Buffett admires the most: high profit margins, high returns on capital, ability to reinvest the profits back into a fast growing company, and management that acts in the interests of shareholders. What we find difficult is estimating the future cash flows of the business so we can then discount back to the present and get some sense of intrinsic value.[20]

"The problem that most people have with trying to value technology companies is that the picture of the future is so uncertain," explains Lisa Rapuano, Vice President and Technology Analyst of Legg Mason Fund Adviser. "So you have to think about several possible outcomes rather than just one. This can create a greater variance in the potential future payoff from a long-term investment. However, if you really dig into the key aspects of the company you're looking at—the potential size of its market, its theoretical profitability, its competitive position—you can understand exactly what is driving the differences between one scenario and another, and that will reduce your uncertainty level. We still create cash flow valuations, but we often use several target values rather than a single one."

Furthermore, says Rapuano, "Since technology is a true driver of future economic growth, and since many winning technology companies generate outsized returns when they do work, we find that the extra level of analysis pays off. It can lead to returns far in excess of what we can find elsewhere, even taking the greater uncertainty into account."[21]

We already know how Warren Buffett, when valuing a company, handles the issue of uncertainty. He requires a larger margin of safety. That is one good strategy for tamping the risk of companies whose future is unclear, like technology companies. Another good strategy is to combine the purchase with a portfolio filled with stable and highly predictable companies.

Buffett is quoted as saying that the next great fortune will be made in identifying what will be the new franchises. "I believe technology companies are the modern-day equivalent of Buffett's franchise factor," argues Bill Miller. In Buffett's consumer products world, brand awareness, pricing power, and share of mind are all factors included in a franchise. In the technology world, the franchise factors include network effects, positive feedbacks, lock-in, and increasing returns.

"I think a lot of people approach technology with a thinking model that is defective," Miller adds. "They believe technology is very difficult to understand so therefore they don't try to understand it. They have already made up their minds in advance."[22] Admittedly, there is a learning curve to understanding technology, but I would argue that becoming accomplished in this field is not the sole domain of computer wizards.

When we first began to study Buffett's cash flow franchise model, we had to switch away from Graham's low price–earnings-ratio and discount-to-book thinking. There were, at the time, new terminology, new definitions, a new way of looking at accounting statements, and the need to understand the dividend discount model. Learning about technology will require the same sort of mental shift. We will have to learn new words and new economic models. We will have to analyze accounting statements somewhat differently. But, in the end, the intellectual challenge is no greater than the switch we made when analyzing how Buffett turned away from the classic value investing (defined as buying only cheap securities) to a modern method of purchasing outstanding companies at reasonable prices.

"It is like anything new," says Miller, "you do have to spend time to understand it." Miller points out that Buffett and Peter Lynch have said that learning is simply a matter of observing what is going on around you. "Yes, people are still buying Coke, and Gillette razor blades, and using their American Express Card," says Miller, "but they are also using America Online, and Microsoft software, and buying Dell Computers—and that's ubiquitous."[23]

SECURITY ANALYSIS REVISITED

Once a week, fifty fourth-term MBA students from the Columbia University Graduate School of Business scramble into Uris Hall to attend a three-hour lecture course titled *Security Analysis*—the same class that Ben Graham taught seventy years ago. Today, the lectures are delivered by Professor Michael Mauboussin. When he is not teaching, Mauboussin spends his time at Crédit Suisse First Boston enlightening his colleagues and the firm's clients.

"Each year, when I stand in front of the class for the first time, I get a lump in my throat," confesses Mauboussin. "I feel an enormous amount of humility trying to perpetuate a tradition which was started by Benjamin Graham and included students like Warren Buffett. There is a tremendous amount of responsibility here."[24]

Mauboussin's lectures encompass three broad concepts. "First," he says, "I emphasize an interdisciplinary approach to investing. Ben Graham was a worldly individual who was able to work into his teachings the ideas from many other disciplines. We attempt to do the same thing. We look not just at finance books, but at other models and metaphors, thinking how they might apply to investing. Second, we try to understand the role of psychology in investing. Ben Graham's Mr. Market is a famous concept and is still valid today. It is important to understand that investing is a social activity and that human psychology plays an important role in the process. Lastly, we talk at length about the 'margin of safety' concept—not only how Ben Graham thought about it but how it can be evidenced in probability statements."[25]

Looking back over the past seventy years, it is amazing to see how the world of investing has changed. The fundamental concepts haven't changed; it is still crucial to buy good financial businesses that are run by able managers and are available at sensible prices. But the economy and the world of business have evolved into quite different forms, and this has required investors to evolve their mental models to keep pace with the changing world.

I asked Professor Mauboussin what advice he would give young people setting forth into the world of investing. "I would first tell them they need to understand the economic models, including not only the accounting numbers and financial statements, but how businesses work and interact as competitors. Second, they would need to understand the role and limitations of human beings in the investment process, and third, I would tell them to work hard, but not too hard."

"Working hard," explained Mauboussin, "means always having your mind working, and reading as much as you can, not only in the financial area but in other areas, to build and fortify the mental models necessary to become successful. When I say don't work too hard, what I mean is there is a tendency to equate activity with getting things done, and in money management it just doesn't work that way. It is very often the people who make fewer but bigger decisions that tend to do better than those who are making a lot of decisions in the name of being busy."

If Ben Graham were alive today, I think he would approve. He surely would feel a great deal of satisfaction about the legacy of *Security Analysis*. Over the years, a distinguished line of professors has taught the course, and many gifted students have profitably applied its lessons to the world they live and work in.

SIX

The Mathematics of Investing

We try to think like Fermat and Pascal [would] if they'd never heard of modern finance theory.

—Charlie Munger

A S A BOY, Warren Buffett was always fascinated with numbers. We already know he invested in common stocks at a young age, but not many people realize that his relationship with numbers goes much further and much deeper than balance sheets and income statements. When he wasn't thinking about the stock market, young Buffett was tackling other mathematical puzzles. Once he decided to calculate whether composers of church hymns lived a longer life than other people.[1] The probabilities of longevity, he learned, are not assigned to the musically gifted.

Today, numbers surround Buffett, and not just stock market numbers. Berkshire's insurance business, which may be the greatest math challenge of all, is also a lesson in statistics and

111

probabilities. When he is not thinking about the insurance business or the stock market, Buffett is often thinking about the numbers in his favorite pastime—bridge. A passionate player since his college days, Buffett spends hours each week playing bridge. When he cannot play in person, he logs onto the Internet and plays with other bridge fanatics scattered across the country.

Buffett sees strong parallels between the game of bridge and investing in the stock market. "It's a game of a million inferences," he explains. "There are a lot of things to draw inferences from—cards played and cards not played. These inferences tell you something about the probabilities. It's got to be the best intellectual exercise out there. You're seeing through new situations every ten minutes. Bridge is about weighing gain/loss ratios," says Buffett. "You're doing calculations all the time."[2]

Anyone who has interacted with Buffett will tell you he has a special gift for quick calculations. Chris Stavrou, a New York money manager and longtime Berkshire Hathaway shareholder, remembers his first meeting with Buffett.[3]

"I asked him whether he ever used a calculator." Buffett replied, "I never owned one and wouldn't know how to use one."

"But how do you do more complicated calculations?" Stavrou pressed. "Are you gifted?"

"No, no," Buffett said. "It's just that I've been working with numbers for a long time. It's number sense."

"Can you give me an example? Like what's 99 times 99?"

Without missing a beat, Buffett replied, "9,801."

Stavrou asked Buffett how he knew that. He answered that he had read Feynman's autobiography.

Richard Feynman, a Nobel laureate in physics, was a member of the U.S. atomic bomb project team. In his autobiography, *Surely You're Joking, Mr. Feynman,* he describes his technique for doing complex math in his head. So of Warren Buffett we can deduce that either (1) he remembers everything he reads, or (2) he can do calculations in his head with lightning speed.

Stavrou pressed for one more example. "If the price of a painting goes from $250 to $50 million in one hundred years, what's the annual rate of return?" Once again Buffett's answer was instantaneous: "13.0 percent." The astonished Stavrou asked, "How did you do that?"

Buffett pointed out that any compound interest table would reveal the answer. (So should we deduce that he's a walking interest table? Maybe.) Another way to approach the problem, said Buffett, was "to go by the number of times it doubles ($250 doubles about 17.6 times to get to $50 million, a double every 5.7 years, or about 13 percent a year)." Simple, he seemed to say.

Despite Buffett's humility, it is clear he is mathematically gifted. For this reason, many skeptics have claimed that Buffett's investment approach works because of this facility, and therefore excludes those who don't have it. Not true, say Buffett and Charlie Munger. To apply Buffett's investment approach does not require investors to learn advanced mathematics. Speaking at a lecture at USC, which was covered by OID, Munger explained, "It's very simple algebra. It's not hard to learn. What is hard is to get so you use it routinely almost every day of your life. The Fermat/Pascal system is dramatically consonant with the way the world works. And it's fundamental truth. So you simply have to have the technique." (OID)[4]

PROBABILITY THEORY

It is a vast oversimplification, but not an overstatement, to say that the stock market is an uncertain universe. In this universe are hundreds, even thousands of single forces that combine to set prices, all of which are constantly in motion, any one of which can have a drastic impact, and none of which is predictable to an absolute certainty. The task for investors, then, is to narrow the field, to identify and remove that which is the most unknown, and to focus on the least unknown. And that is an exercise in probability.

When we are unsure about a situation but still want to express our opinion, we often preface our remarks with: "The chances are," or "Probably," or "It's not very likely." When we go one step further and attempt to quantify those general expressions, we then are dealing with probabilities. Probabilities are the mathematical language of uncertainty.

What is the probability of a cat's giving birth to a bird? Zero. What is the probability the sun will rise tomorrow? That event, which is considered certain, is given a probability of one. All events that are neither certain nor impossible have a probability that is a fraction somewhere between 0 and 1.0. Determining the fraction is what probability theory is all about.

In 1654, Blaise Pascal and Pierre de Fermat exchanged a series of letters that formed the basis of what today is probability theory. Pascal, a child prodigy gifted both in mathematics and philosophy, had been challenged by Chevalier de Méré, a philosopher and gambler, to solve the riddle that had stumped many a mathematician. De Méré wanted to know how two card players should divide the stakes of a game if they had to leave before the game was completed. Pascal approached Fermat, a mathematical genius in his own right, about de Méré's challenge.

"The 1654 correspondence between Pascal and Fermat on this subject," says Peter Bernstein in *Against the Gods,* his wonderfully written treatise on risk, "signaled an epochal event in the history of mathematics and the theory of probability."[5] Although they attacked the problem differently (Fermat used algebra whereas Pascal turned to geometry), they were able to construct a system to determine the probability of several possible outcomes. Indeed, Pascal's triangle of numbers solves many problems, including the probability of your favorite baseball team's winning the World Series after losing the first game.

The work by Pascal and Fermat marks the beginning of the theory of decision making. Decision theory is the process of deciding what to do when you are uncertain what will happen. "Making that decision," writes Bernstein, "is the essential first step in any effort to manage risk."[6] Although Pascal and Fermat are both credited with developing probability theory, another mathematician, Thomas Bayes, wrote the piece that laid the groundwork for putting it into practical action.

Born in England in 1701, exactly one hundred years after Fermat and seventy-eight years after Pascal, Bayes lived an unremarkable life. He was a member of the Royal Society, but published nothing in mathematics during his lifetime. After his death, his paper entitled "Essays Towards Solving A Problem In The Doctrine Of Chances" appeared. At the time, no one thought much of it. However, according to Peter Bernstein, Bayes's essay was a "strikingly original piece of work that immortalized Bayes among statisticians, economists, and other social scientists."[7] It provides a way for investors to make use of the mathematical theory of probability.

Bayesian analysis gives us a logical way to consider a set of outcomes of which all are possible but only one will actually occur. It is conceptually a simple procedure. We begin by assigning a probability to each of the outcomes on the basis of whatever evidence is then available. If additional evidence becomes available, the initial probability is revised to reflect the new information.

Bayes's theorem thus gives us a mathematical procedure for updating our original beliefs (which had resulted from what he called a prior distribution of information) to produce a posterior distribution of information. In other words, prior probabilities combined with new information yield posterior probabilities and thus change our relevant odds.

How does it work?

Let's imagine that you and a friend have spent the afternoon playing your favorite board game, and now, at the end of the game, are chatting about this and that. Something your friend says leads you to make a friendly wager: that with one roll of the die from the board game, you will get a 6. Straight odds are one in six, a 16 percent probability. But then suppose your friend rolls the die, quickly covers it with her hand, and takes a peek. "I can tell you this much," she says; "it's an even number." With this new information, your odds change to one in three, a 33 percent probability. While you consider whether to change your bet, your friend teasingly adds: "And it's not a 4." With this additional bit of information, your odds have changed again, to one in two, a 50 percent probability.

With this very simple sequence, you have performed a Bayesian analysis. Each new piece of information affected the original probability, and that is a Bayesian inference.

Bayesian analysis is an attempt to incorporate all available information into a process for making inferences, or decisions, about the underlying state of nature. Colleges and universities use Bayes's theorem to help their students study decision making. In the classroom, the Bayesian approach is more popularly called the decision tree theory, in which each branch of the tree represents new information that, in turn, changes the odds in making decisions. "At Harvard Business School," explains Charlie Munger, "the great quantitative thing that bonds the first-year class together is what they call decision tree theory. All they do is take high school algebra and apply it to real-life problems. The students love it. They're amazed to find that high school algebra works in life." (OID)[8]

THE SUBJECTIVE INTERPRETATION OF PROBABILITY

As Charlie points out, basic algebra is extremely useful in calculating probabilities. But to put probability theory to practical use in investing, we need to look a bit deeper at how the numbers are calculated. In particular, we need to pay attention to the notion of frequency.

What does it mean to say that the probability of guessing heads on a single coin toss is 1/2? Or that the probability of an odd number's appearing on a single throw of a die is 1/2? If a box is filled with seventy red marbles and thirty blue marbles, what does it mean that the probability is 3/10 that a blue marble will be picked? In all these examples, the probability of the event is what is referred to as a frequency interpretation, and it is based on the law of averages.

If an uncertain event is repeated countless times, the frequency of the event's occurrence is reflected in the probability of the event. For example, if we toss a coin 100,000 times, the number of events that are expected to be heads is 50,000. Note that I did not say it *would be* equal to 50,000. The law of large numbers says the relative frequency and the probability need be equal only for an infinite number of repetitions. Theoretically, we know that in a fair toss of a coin the chance of getting a "head" is 1/2, but we will never be able to say the chance is equal until an infinite number of tosses has passed.

In any problem that deals with uncertainty, we will, quite obviously, never be able to make a definitive statement. However, if the problem is well defined, we should be able to list all the possible outcomes. If an uncertain event is repeated often enough, the frequency of the outcomes should reflect the probability of the different possible outcomes. The difficulty arises when we are concerned with an event that happens only once.

How do we estimate the probability of passing tomorrow's science test or the probability of the Green Bay Packers' recapturing the Super Bowl championship? The problem we face is that each of these events is unique. We can look back at all the stats on the Green Bay games, but we don't have enough exact match-ups with the exact personnel who played each other repeatedly under identical circumstances. We can recall previous science exams to get an idea of how well we test, but all tests are not identical and our knowledge is not constant.

Without repeated tests that would produce a frequency distribution, how can we calculate probability? We cannot. Instead, we must rely on a *subjective* interpretation of probabilities. We do it all the time. We might say that the odds of the Packers' recapturing the big prize are 2 to 1, or the possibility of passing that hard test is 1 in 10. These are probabilistic statements; they describe our "degree of belief" about the event. When it isn't possible to do enough repetitions of a certain event to get an interpretation of probability based on frequency, we have to rely on our own good sense.

You can immediately see that many subjective interpretations of those two events would lead you in the wrong direction. In subjective probability, the burden is on you to analyze your assumptions. Stop and think through your situation. Are you assuming a one-in-ten chance of doing well on the science test because the material is difficult and you haven't adequately prepared, or because of false modesty? Is your lifelong loyalty to the Packers blinding you to the superior strength of the other teams?

According to the textbooks on Bayesian analysis, if you believe that your assumptions are reasonable, it is "perfectly acceptable" to make your subjective probability of a certain event equal to a frequency probability.[9] What you have to do is sift out the unreasonable and illogical in favor of the reasonable. It is helpful if you think about subjective probabilities as nothing more than an extension of the frequency probability method. In fact, in many cases, subjective probabilities are value added because this approach allows you to take operational issues into account rather than depend on long-run statistical regularity.

Whether or not they recognize it, virtually all decisions that investors make are exercises in probability. For them to succeed, it is critical that their probability statement combines the historical record with the most recent data available. And that is Bayesian analysis in action.

PROBABILITIES, BUFFETT STYLE

"Take the probability of loss times the amount of possible loss from the probability of gain times the amount of possible gain. That is what we're trying to do," says Buffett. "It's imperfect, but that's what it is all about."[10]

A useful example to clarify the link between investing and probability theory is the practice of risk arbitrage. As reported by OID, Buffett shared his views on risk arbitrage with a group of Stanford students. "Risk arbitrage is something I've been doing for forty years now," explained Buffett. "And my boss Ben

Graham did it for thirty years before that." (OID)[11] A pure arbitrage is nothing more than profiting from the discrepancy in the price of a security quoted in two different markets. For example, commodities and currencies are quoted in several different markets around the world. If two separate markets quoted a different price on the same commodity, you could buy in one market, sell in the other market, and pocket the difference.

Risk arbitrage, which is the form more commonly practiced today, involves announced corporate mergers or acquisitions. (Some speculators practice risk arbitrage on unannounced corporate events, but this is an area that Buffett avoids and so shall we.) "My job," says Buffett, "is to assess the probability of the events [announced mergers] actually transpiring and the gain/loss ratio." (OID)[12]

Let's preface Buffett's next remarks with this scenario. Suppose the Abbott Company began the trading day at $18 per share. Then, in midmorning, it is announced that sometime this year, perhaps in six months, Abbott will be sold to the Costello Company for $30 per share. Immediately, the share price of Abbott races to $27, where it settles in and begins to trade back and forth.

Buffett sees the announced merger and must make a decision. First, he tries to assess the degree of certainty. Some corporate deals don't materialize. The board of directors could unexpectedly resist the idea of a merger, or the Federal Trade Commission might voice an objection. No one ever knows with certainty whether a risk arbitrage deal will close, and that is where the risk comes in.

Buffett's decision process is an exercise in subjective probability. He explains: "If I think an event has a 90 percent chance of occurring and there is 3 points on the upside, and there is a 10 percent chance that it will fall through, and there's 9 points on the downside, then that's $.90 off of $2.70 leaving $1.80 mathematical expectation." (OID)[13]

Next, says Buffett, you have to figure in the time span involved, and then relate the return of the investment to other investments available to you. If you bought one share of Abbott Company at $27, according to Buffett's mathematics there is a potential 6.6 percent return ($1.80/$27). If the deal was expected to close in six months, the annualized return on the investment would be 13.2 percent. Buffett would then compare the return from this risk arbitrage with other returns available to him.

Risk arbitrage carries the potential for loss. "We're perfectly willing to lose money on a given transaction—arbitrage being one example—but we're not willing to enter into any transaction in which we think the probability of a number of mutually independent events of a similar type has an expectancy of loss. We hope," confesses Buffett, "that we're entering into transactions where our calculations of those probabilities have validity." (OID)[14]

We can see quite clearly that Buffett's risk arbitrage estimates are subjective probabilities. There is no frequency distribution in risk arbitrage. Every deal is different. Every circumstance requires different estimations. Even so, there is value to approaching the risk arbitrage deal with some rational mathematical calculation.

The process is no different for an investment in common stocks. To illustrate this, let's look at two classic Berkshire Hathaway common stock purchases—Wells Fargo and Coca-Cola.

INVESTING IN WELLS FARGO
AND COCA-COLA

In October 1990, Berkshire Hathaway purchased 5 million shares of Wells Fargo & Company, investing $289 million in the company at an average price of $57.88 per share.[15] With this purchase, Berkshire became the largest shareholder of the bank, owning 10 percent of the shares outstanding.

It was a very controversial move. Earlier in the year, the share price had traded as high as $86, then dropped sharply as investors abandoned California banks in droves. At the time, the West Coast was in the throes of a severe recession, and some speculated that banks, with their loan portfolios filled with commercial and residential mortgages, were in trouble. Wells Fargo, with the most commercial real estate of any California bank, was thought to be particularly vulnerable.

Buffett was well aware of what was being said, but he came to a different conclusion about Wells Fargo. Did he know something that other investment professionals did not? Not really. He just analyzed the situation differently. Let's walk through the thinking process with him, for it gives us a clear example of how Buffett uses probabilities.

First, Buffett understood the banking business very well. Berkshire had owned the Illinois National Bank and Trust Company between 1969 and 1979. During that period, Gene Abegg, chairman of Illinois National, had taught Buffett that a well-managed bank could not only grow its earnings but also earn a handsome return on equity. Importantly, Buffett also learned that the long-term value of a bank is determined by the actions of its management. Bad managers have a way of running up the costs of operations while making foolish loans; good managers are always looking for ways to cut costs, and they very rarely make risky loans.

Carl Reichardt, then chairman of Wells Fargo, had run the bank since 1983, with impressive results. Under his leadership, growth in earnings and return on equity were above average, and operating efficiencies were among the highest in the country. Reichardt had also built a solid loan portfolio.

"Ownership of a bank is far from riskless," said Buffett.[16] However, in his mind, the risk of owning Wells Fargo centered around three possibilities:

"California banks face the specific risk of a major earthquake, which might wreak havoc on borrowers that in turn destroy the banks lending to them.

"A second risk is systemic—the possibility of a business contraction or financial panic so severe it would endanger almost every highly leveraged institution, no matter how intelligently run.

"The market's major fear of the moment is that West Coast real estate values will tumble because of overbuilding and deliver huge losses to banks that have financed the expansion."[17]

Now, Buffett said, none of these scenarios can be ruled out. However, he concluded, based on best evidence, that the probability of an earthquake or a severe financial panic was low. (Buffett gives us no figures, but a "low" probability might be something less than 10 percent.)

Then he turned his attention to the probability of the third scenario. He reasoned that a meaningful drop in real estate values should not cause major problems for a well-managed bank like Wells Fargo. "Consider some mathematics," explains Buffett. "Wells Fargo currently earns well over $1 billion pretax annually after expensing more than $300 million for loan losses. If 10 percent of all $48 billion of the bank's loans—not just its real estate loans—were hit by problems in 1991, and these produced losses (including forgone interest) averaging 30 percent of principal, the company would roughly break even." Now consider that a 10 percent loss in a bank's portfolio would certainly qualify as a severe business contraction, which Buffett had already rated a "low" possibility. But even if that were to occur, the bank would still break even. Buffett continued, "A year like that— which we consider only a low-level possibility, not a likelihood— would not distress us."[18]

In the multiple scenarios that Buffett mentally laid out, the probability of any major long-lasting damage to Wells Fargo was, at best, low. Still, the market priced Wells Fargo's shares down by 50 percent. In Buffett's mind, the odds of making money by purchasing shares of Wells Fargo were now in the order of 2:1, with no corresponding increase in the probabilities of being wrong.

Although Buffett doesn't assign specific numbers to his probability statements, that doesn't lessen the value of his thought process. Thinking in probabilities, subjective or not, enables you to think clearly and rationally about a purchase. The way Buffett rationalized Wells Fargo allowed him to act and profit when others were thinking less clearly. Remember, says Buffett, "If you believe that your gain, weighted for probabilities, considerably exceeds your loss, comparably weighted, you may consciously purchase a risky investment."[19]

Coca-Cola is a different story. If Wells Fargo allows us to watch Buffett spread out multiple scenarios and assign various probabilities to them, Coca-Cola lets us see what he does when he thinks the probabilities are practically dead certain. In the case of Coca-Cola, we see Buffett acting on one of his guiding principles: When the probabilities of success are very high, make a big bet.

Buffett does not walk us through a Bayesian analysis of his purchase of Coca-Cola. However, he has often said that Coca-Cola represented a near certain probability of success. With over a hundred years of investment performance data available, Coca-Cola had something very close to a frequency distribution to analyze. Then, using the Bayesian process, which adds posterior information, Buffett could see the difference that Roberto Goizueta's management was making. Because Goizueta was selling the poor-performing businesses and reinvesting the proceeds in the higher-performing syrup business, Buffett knew the financial returns of Coca-Cola were going to improve. In addition, Goizueta was buying back shares of Coca-Cola in the market, thereby increasing the economic value of the business even more.

Starting in 1988, Buffett could see that the market was pricing Coca-Cola somewhere between 50 percent and 70 percent below its intrinsic value. At the same time, his conviction about the company had not changed: the probabilities of Coca-Cola's share price beating the market rate of return were going up, up, and up. So what did Buffett do? Between 1988 and 1989, Berkshire Hathaway purchased $1 billion of Coca-Cola stock, an amount that came to represent over 30 percent of the total value of Berkshire's portfolio. By year-end 1998, that investment was worth over $13 billion.

THE KELLY OPTIMIZATION MODEL

Each time you set foot inside a casino, the probability of coming out a winner is pretty low. You shouldn't be surprised; we all know the house has the best odds. But one game, if played correctly, gives you a legitimate chance to beat the house—blackjack. In a worldwide best seller called *Beat the Dealer: A Winning Strategy for the Game of Twenty-One,* Edward O. Thorp, a mathematician by training, outlined a process for outsmarting the casino.[20]

Thorp's strategy was based on a simple concept. When the deck is rich with 10s, face cards, and aces, the player—let's say it's you—has a statistical advantage over the dealer. If you assign a −1 for the high cards and a +1 for the low cards, it's quite easy to keep track of the cards dealt; just keep a running tally in your head, adding or subtracting as each card shows. When the count turns positive, you know there are more high cards yet to be played. Smart players would save their biggest bets for when the card count reached a high relative number.

Buried deep inside Thorp's book was a notation on the Kelly betting model.[21] Kelly, in turn, took his inspiration from Claude Shannon, the inventor of information theory.

A mathematician with Bell Laboratories in the 1940s, Shannon spent a good part of his career trying to find the most optimal way to transmit information over copper lines without having the information become garbled by random molecular noise. In 1948, in an article called "A Mathematical Theory of Communication," he described what he had discovered.[22] Inside the paper was the mathematical formula for the optimal amount of information that, considering the possibilities of success, can be pushed through copper wire.

A few years later, J. L. Kelly, another mathematician, read Shannon's article and realized that the formula could just as easily work in gambling—another human endeavor that would be enhanced by knowing the possibilities of success. In 1956, in a paper entitled "A New Interpretation of Information Rate," Kelly pointed out that Shannon's various transmission rates and the possible outcomes of a chance event are essentially the same thing—probabilities—and the same formula could optimize both.[23]

The Kelly Optimization Model, often called the optimal growth strategy, is based on the concept that if you know the probability of success, you bet the fraction of your bankroll that maximizes the growth rate. It is expressed as a formula:

$$2p - 1 = x$$

where 2 times the probability of winning minus 1 equals the percentage of one's bankroll that should be bet. For example, if the probability of beating the house is 55 percent, you should bet 10 percent of your bankroll to achieve maximum growth of your winnings. If the probability is 70 percent, bet 40 percent. And if you know the odds of winning are 100 percent, the model would say, bet your entire bankroll.

The Kelly formula is optimal under two criteria: (1) the minimal expected time to achieve a level of winnings and (2) the maximal rate of wealth increase. For example, let's say two blackjack players each have a $1,000 stake and twenty-four hours to play it. The first player is limited to betting only $1 on each hand dealt; player number two can alter the bet, depending on the attractiveness of the cards. If the second player follows the Kelly approach and bets the percentage of his bankroll that reflects the probability of winning, it is likely that, at the end of twenty-four hours, he will have done much better than player number one.

The stock market, of course, is far more complex than the game of blackjack, in which there is a finite number of cards and therefore a limited number of possible outcomes. The market, with hundreds of common stocks and millions of investors, has an almost unlimited number of outcomes. Using the Kelly approach requires constant recalculations and adjustments throughout the investment process. Nonetheless, the underlying concept—mathematically linking degree of probability to investment size—carries important lessons for the focus investor.

Let's revisit our two gamblers and their twenty-four-hour clock. Instead of playing blackjack, they are now investing in the stock market. Investor number one is limited to investing only 1 percent of the portfolio on each event; the second investor is allowed to alter the investment, depending on how he perceives the probability of success. Which investor stands the better chance of optimally growing capital over the marking period, the investor who bets 1 percent on each event knowing that not every stock is an equally weighted opportunity, or the focus investor who waits until the high probability event appears and then bets big?

We have no evidence that Buffett uses the Kelly model when allocating Berkshire's capital. But the Kelly concept is a rational process and, to my mind, it neatly echoes Buffett's thinking. Buffett has counseled investors to wait until the best opportunities appear and then be willing to bet big. In any event, I have found the Kelly model useful as a mathematical explanation that yields a better understanding of the portfolio allocation process.

I believe the Kelly model is an attractive tool for focus investors. However, it will benefit only those who use it responsibly. There are risks attached to employing the Kelly approach, and you would be wise to understand its three limitations.

First, anyone who intends to invest, using the Kelly model or not, should have a long-term horizon. Even if a blackjack player has a sound model that can beat the house, success will not always be revealed in the first few hands dealt. The same is true for investing. How many times have investors seen that they have selected the right company but the market has taken its own sweet time in rewarding the selection?

Second, be wary of using leverage. The danger of borrowing to invest in the stock market (with a margin account) has been trumpeted loudly by both Ben Graham and Warren Buffett. The unexpected call on your capital can occur at the most unfortunate time in the game. If you use the Kelly model in a margin account, a stock market decline can force you to remove your high-probability bets.

Third, the biggest danger in playing high-probability games is the risk of overbetting. If you judge an event has a 70 percent probability of success when in fact it is only 55 percent, you run the risk of "gambler's ruin." The way to minimize that risk is underbetting—using a half-Kelly or a fractional-Kelly model. This increases the safety of your bet and provides a very real psychological level of comfort. For example, if the Kelly model would tell you to bet 10 percent of your capital (indicating the event has a 55 percent probability of success), you might choose to invest only 5 percent (a half-Kelly) instead. The fractional Kelly provides a margin of safety in portfolio management; that, together with the margin of safety we apply to selecting individual stocks, provides a double layer of protection.

Because the risk of overbetting far outweighs the penalties of underbetting, investors—particularly those who are just beginning to use a focus investment strategy—should use fractional Kelly bets. Unfortunately, minimizing your bets also minimizes your potential gain. However, because the relationship in the Kelly model is parabolic, the penalty for underbetting is not severe. A half-Kelly, which reduces the amount of the bet by 50 percent, reduces the potential growth rate by only 25 percent.

This seems a good place to summarize:

1. To receive the benefit of the Kelly model, you must first be willing to think about buying stocks in terms of probabilities.
2. You must be willing to play the game long enough to achieve its rewards.
3. You must avoid using leverage, with its unfortunate consequence.
4. You should demand a margin of safety with each bet you make.

"The Kelly system is for people who simply want to compound their capital and see it grow to very large numbers over time," says Ed Thorp. "If you have a lot of time and a lot of patience, then it's the right function for you."[24]

INSURANCE IS LIKE INVESTING

"Insurance is a lot like investing," explains Buffett. "If you feel like you have to invest every day, you're going to make a lot of mistakes." To succeed in investing or in writing insurance, "You have to wait for the fat pitch." (OID)[25]

Warren Buffett has been in the insurance game since 1967—the year in which Berkshire Hathaway purchased National Indemnity Company. Since then, Buffett has acquired several more insurance businesses, including GEICO and, most recently, General Re Corporation. GEICO is a direct writer of automobile insurance. Because the company sells insurance directly to the customer, bypassing the need for agents, GEICO has become the low-cost provider of insurance and now stands ready to take a large segment of the $100 billion automobile insurance market. General Re, in a $16 billion merger that was completed at the end of 1998, makes Berkshire Hathaway the largest worldwide provider of super-catastrophe ("super-cat") reinsurance.

Super-catastrophe insurance policies are purchased by primary insurance companies that wish to protect themselves from the financial damage caused by natural disasters—principally, hurricanes or earthquakes. Typically, a primary insurer may choose to retain the loss from a single catastrophic event up to a certain level and then reinsure through another carrier for any damages above that threshold. Berkshire Hathaway provides insurance for these super-catastrophes by insuring not only primary carriers but other reinsurance companies that wish to lay off the most severe possibility.

Pricing super-catastrophe insurance is a tricky business because frequency distributions and precise data are unavailable. (Earthquakes and hurricanes do not occur often enough to build reliable statistics; by comparison, automobile insurance can rely on the law of large numbers.) "Catastrophe insurers can't simply extrapolate past experience," says Buffett. "If there is truly 'global warming,' for example, the odds would shift, since tiny changes in atmospheric conditions can produce momentous changes in weather patterns." Furthermore, says Buffett, "In recent years there has been a mushrooming of population and insured values in U.S. coastal areas that are particularly vulnerable to hurricanes, the number-one creator of super-cats. A hurricane that caused x dollars of damage twenty years ago could easily cost $10x$ now."[26]

Because of the difficulty of predicting when an earthquake or a hurricane is going to hit, you might assume that estimating the probabilities of these events is a total crapshoot. Not so, says Buffett. "Even if perfection in assessing risks is unattainable, insurers can underwrite sensibly. After all, you need not know a man's precise age to know if he is old enough to vote nor know his exact weight to recognize his need to diet," explains Buffett.[27] It is not a perfect science, and uncertainty of this type might cause other people to have some concerns; but not Buffett. "What I can say with certainty," says Buffett, "is that we have the best person in the world to run our super-cat business: Ajit Jain, whose value to Berkshire Hathaway is simply enormous."[28]

Ajit is the "guiding genius" and developer of Berkshire's super-cat business. Born in India and educated at Harvard Business School, Ajit worked for both IBM and McKinsey Consulting before joining Berkshire Hathaway's National Indemnity. Ajit had the foresight to see the growing need for large super-catastrophe insurance policies, and he recognized that Berkshire's financial strength gave it a competitive advantage.

Like Buffett, Ajit is keenly aware of the need for skill in making subjective interpretations of probability. "The reality in the super-catastrophe business is that there isn't a lot of meaningful data to analyze. What you do is start with historical data and then you make certain projections from that. It's a very subjective art form."[29]

The super-catastrophe insurance business is a perfect example of an environment of low-frequency, high-severity events. So is focus investing. The focus investor, remember, makes very few bets but always on high-probability situations. If managed properly, the focus portfolio will have a low frequency of failure, but when failure does occur it will be severe. The portfolio will take a larger-than-normal hit.

I had the opportunity to ask Charlie Munger about the similarities between focus investing and super-catastrophe insurance. He smiled and told me, "The thinking is identical."[30] If so, the history of super-catastrophe insurance will give us a sense of what focus investors can expect. "By its nature," says Buffett, "the super-cat business is the most volatile of all insurance lines. Since truly major catastrophes are rare occurrences, our super-cat business can be expected to show large profits in most years—and to record a huge loss occasionally. What you must understand, however, is that a truly terrible year in the super-cat business is not a possibility—it's a certainty. The only question is when it will come."[31]

Large profits in most years, occasional huge losses, and a truly terrible year at some point—that profile could easily describe the focus investing style as well as super-catastrophe insurance. (Think back to the performance history of our focus investors in Chapter 4: Keynes, Munger, Ruane, and Simpson.) With the potential for such losses, why does Buffett promote the super-cat insurance business? For the same reason he embraced the focus approach.

"We will get hit from time to time with large losses," explains Buffett. "Charlie and I, however, are quite willing to accept relatively volatile results in exchange for better long-term earnings than we would otherwise have had. Since most managers opt for smoothness, we are left with a competitive advantage that we try to maximize. In other words, we prefer the lumpy 15 percent to a smooth 12 percent."[32]

IT'S ALL ABOUT ODDS

"The model I like—to sort of simplify the notion of what goes on in a market for common stocks—is the pari-mutuel system at the racetrack," as Charlie explained at a USC lecture featured in OID. "If you stop to think about it, a pari-mutuel system is a market. Everybody goes there and bets and the odds are changed based on what's bet. That's what happens in the stock market." (OID)[33]

Continuing this line of reasoning, Charlie explains as only he can. "Any damn fool can see that a horse carrying a light weight with a wonderful win rate and good position etc. is way more likely to win than a horse with a terrible record and extra weight and so on and so on. But if you look at the odds, the bad horse pays 100 to 1, whereas the good horse pays 3 to 2. Then it's not clear which is statistically the best bet. The prices have changed in such a way that it's very hard to beat the system." (OID)[34]

Charlie's racetrack analogy is perfect for investors. Too often, investors are attracted to a long shot that pays incredible odds but, for any one of countless reasons, never wins the race. Or, investors sometimes pick the sure thing without ever considering the payoff. It appears to me that the most sensible way to approach horse racing or the stock market is to lie back and wait until the good horse comes to the post with the inviting odds.

Andrew Beyer, columnist for *The Washington Post* and author of several books on thoroughbred racing, has spent many years watching racegoers bet, and has seen far too many lose money through impetuosity. At the track, as elsewhere, the casino mentality—the itch to get into the action; to put down the money, toss the dice, pull the lever, do *something*—compels people to bet foolishly, without taking the time to think through what they are doing.

Beyer, who understands this psychological urge to get in the game, advises players to accommodate it by dividing their strategy between action bets and prime bets. Prime bets are reserved for serious plays when two conditions occur: (1) confidence in the horse's ability to win is high, and (2) payoff odds are greater than they should be. Prime bets call for serious money. Action bets, as the name implies, are reserved for the long shots and hunches that satisfy the psychological need to play. They are smaller bets and are never allowed to become a large part of the player's betting pool.

When a horseplayer starts blurring the distinction between prime bets and action bets, says Beyer, he is "taking a step that will inevitably lead toward helter-skelter betting with no proper balance between his strong and weak selections."[35]

A NEW WAY OF THINKING

If the whole idea of applying mathematics and probability calculations to investment decisions seems intimidating, you are not alone. As Charlie Munger once remarked, most people "are total klutzes at dealing with ordinary probabilities and numbers." (OID)[36] Is it worth the effort? Without doubt.

Perhaps it will be helpful if we step back for a moment and look at the big picture, reviewing what we have learned in this chapter.

One of the first things we notice when we examine Warren Buffett's approach to managing a portfolio is that he believes in making big bets on high-probability events. That leads us to the first question: What is probability, and how do we determine it?

Calculating Probability

If the circumstance you're investigating has only a limited number of possible outcomes, calculating probability is a matter of simple arithmetic. A die has only six sides, so the probability of any one of them landing face up is one in six.

If the number of possible outcomes is unlimited, and if, looking backward, you can find a large number of instances, then you can conclude probability on the basis of a frequency distribution. This is how we predict long-range weather patterns, and it is how carriers of automobile insurance establish rates for different classes of drivers.

If the number of possible outcomes is unlimited but you do not have access to enough repetitions to make a frequency distribution, then you must do a subjective interpretation, collecting as much information as you can and analyzing it thoughtfully. In this case, your probability determination coincides with your level of confidence in your analysis.

Using any of these variations, you end up with a determination of the chances that the particular event will happen, expressed as a percentage: 50 percent, 70 percent, whatever.

This is your estimate of probability, based on your best information at the time. But what happens if new information becomes available?

Adjusting a Calculation to Integrate New Information

Suppose new information comes in, and suppose it clearly suggests that the situation might have more than one outcome, depending on various circumstances. You are then faced with a decision tree: If X happens, the probability of success is

55 percent, but if Y happens, the probability would change to 70 percent.

This is a Bayesian analysis. Your answer is more complex because it has several variations, but the process is the same: Take each variation, gather all the data you can, and think it through as thoroughly as you can. Then you have a probability calculation for each of the possible outcomes. Yes, it helps if you are quick with numbers, but it is not a necessary talent.

Now that we know the probability, as much as it is knowable, we are ready for the second question: How much should you bet—in other words, how big is big?

Determining the Size of the Bet

The Kelly Optimization Model will tell you how much to bet, expressed as a fraction of the total. When the situation is fluid and complex, as it is in the stock market, you may not be able to apply the formula rigidly. You will have to make allowance for the continually shifting forces. The basic notion still applies: As the probability rises, so should the amount of the investment.

Now we have two big pieces of the picture: probability and investment size. One question remains: When should you make your move? Not until the odds are in your favor.

Watching the Odds

The horse that is favored to win the race has the highest probability, but might not be a good bet if the odds are only 3 to 2; the profit potential is not particularly exciting. But if your information leads you to believe that another horse also has a high probability of winning, and the odds are more favorable, that's when you make your big bet.

PROBABILITY THEORY AND THE MARKET

Now, let us move away from the racetrack, and away from theory, and put this all together into the reality of the stock market. The chain of thinking is the same.

1. *Calculate probabilities.* As a focus investor, you restrict yourself to a limited number of stocks because you know that, in the long run, it is your best chance of doing better than the overall market. So, when thinking about buying a new stock, your goal is to make sure your choice will outperform the market. That is the probability you are concerned with: What are the chances that this stock, over time, will achieve an economic return greater than the market?

Using frequency if it is available, and subjective interpretation if it is not, make your best estimate. What you will be looking at is how closely the company you are considering matches up to the tenets of the Warren Buffett Way (see box in Chapter 1). Do the most thorough job you can of collecting information about the company. Measure it against those tenets, and convert your analysis to a number. That number represents how obvious it is to you that the company is a winner.

2. *Adjust for new information.* Knowing that you are going to wait until the odds turn in your favor, pay scrupulous attention to whatever the company does. Is management beginning to act irresponsibly? Are the financial decisions beginning to change? Has something happened to change the competitive landscape in which the business operates? If so, the probabilities will likely change.

3. *Decide how much to invest.* Out of all the funds you have available for investing in the market, what proportion should go to this particular purchase? Start with the Kelly formula, then adjust it downward, perhaps by half.

4. *Wait for the best odds.* The odds of success tip in your favor when you have a margin of safety; the more uncertain the situation, the greater margin you need. In the stock market, that safety margin is provided by a discounted price. When the company you like is selling at a price that is below its intrinsic value (which you have determined in the process of analyzing probabilities), that is your signal to act.

It will be obvious, I'm sure, that this process is a continuous loop. As the circumstances change, the probabilities change; with new probabilities, you might need a new margin of safety, and so you have to adjust your sense of what constitutes the best odds. If this seems too difficult, think about the hundreds of small choices you make every time you drive your car, constantly adjusting your actions in response to the situation around you. The stakes are much higher—your safety and others'—yet you make these changes almost without conscious thought. In comparison, keeping up with a few companies is relatively easy. It is simply a matter of experience.

"It's not given to human beings to have such talent that they can just know everything about everything all the time," says Charlie. "But it is given to human beings who work hard at it— who look and sift the world for a mispriced bet—that they can occasionally find one." Furthermore, says Charlie, "The wise ones bet heavily when the world offers them that opportunity. They bet big when they have the odds. And the rest of the time, they don't. It's just that simple." (OID)[37]

THE BEAUTY OF NUMBERS

The world is full of people who love numbers, who view pure mathematics with the same reverence other people hold for classical music or beautifully crafted antique furniture. For them, talking of probability calculations is a joy unto itself.

For everyone else, mathematics is simply a tool for getting things done or for increasing understanding. And, like all tools, the mathematics in this chapter takes some getting used to. The more practice you have with using it, the easier it becomes.

"You have to learn in a very usable way this elementary math and use it routinely in life," says Charlie. "If you don't get this elementary, but mildly unnatural, mathematics of elementary probability into your repertoire, then you go through a long life like a one-legged man in an ass-kicking contest. You're giving a huge advantage to everybody else." (OID)[38]

Without question, Buffett's success is tied closely to numbers. "One of the advantages of a fellow like Buffett whom I've worked for all these years," confesses Charlie, "is that he automatically thinks in terms of decision trees and the elementary math of permutations and combinations." (OID)[39] Most people do not. It doesn't appear that the majority of investors are psychologically predisposed to thinking in multiple scenarios. We have a tendency to make decisions categorically while ignoring the probabilities.

Thinking in probabilities is not impossible; it simply requires attacking the problem in a different manner. Furthermore, if your investing assumptions do not express statistical probabilities, it's likely your conclusions are emotionally biased. And emotions, as we will see in the next chapter, have a way of leading us in the wrong direction, especially emotions about money.

But if you are able to teach yourself to think in probabilities, you are well on your way to being able to profit from your own lessons. Not often will the market price Coca-Cola or any other outstanding businesses substantially below their intrinsic value. But when it does occur, you should be financially and psychologically prepared to bet big. In the meantime, you should continue to study stocks as businesses with the idea that one day the market will give you compelling odds on a good investment. "Considering what it takes to be an Inevitable," says Buffett, "Charlie and I recognize we will never be able to come up with a Nifty Fifty or even a Twinkling Twenty. To the Inevitables in our portfolio, therefore, we add a few Highly Probables."[40]

SEVEN

The Psychology
of Investing

*I came to the psychology of misjudgment almost against
my will; I rejected it until I realized my attitude was
costing me a lot of money.*

—Charlie Munger

PSYCHOLOGY—THE TWISTS and turns of human behavior—has no place in the efficient market hypothesis and
modern portfolio theory. According to its advocates, market efficiency occurs because investors, with the benefit of full information, instantly and rationally set prices.

But since when are people rational about money?

Few aspects of human existence are more emotion-laden
than our relationship to money. We make more emotional, illogical decisions about financial matters than we do about practically any other activity of our lives. Attempting to develop
financial understanding without taking into account the human

factor is like trying to navigate with a compass but no map: you have ignored half the formula.

It is particularly important to include the human factor when we are talking about the stock market. The more abstract the environment—and stocks are an abstraction to many people—the more forceful the intangible psychological factors become. As we will see, much of what drives the decisions that people make about stock purchases can be explained only by principles of human behavior. And because the market is, by definition, the collective decisions made by all stock purchasers, it is not an exaggeration to say that the entire market is pushed and pulled by psychological forces.

The efficient market theory has been accepted as valid so strongly and for so long that any discussion of markets that included psychological concepts was met with, at best, patronizing attitudes. Until recently, that is. In the past few years, we have seen what amounts to a revolution, a new way of looking at issues of finance through the framework of human behavior. This blending of economics and psychology is known as behavioral finance, and it is just now moving down from the universities' ivory towers to become part of the informed conversation among investment professionals . . . who, if they look over their shoulders, will find the shadow of a smiling Ben Graham.

BENJAMIN GRAHAM

Ben Graham, widely known as the Father of Financial Analysis, taught three generations how to navigate the stock market. His value investing approach has helped, without exaggeration, hundreds of thousands of people pick stocks. But often overlooked are Graham's teachings on psychology and investing. In both

Security Analysis and *The Intelligent Investor,* Graham devoted considerable space to explaining how investors' emotions triggered stock market fluctuations.

Graham figured that an investor's worst enemy was not the stock market but oneself. Despite superior abilities in mathematics, finance, and accounting, people who could not master their emotions were ill suited to profit from the investment process.

As Warren Buffett, his most famous student, explains, "There are three important principles to Graham's approach." The first is simply looking at stocks as businesses, which "gives you an entirely different view than most people who are in the market." The second principle is the margin-of-safety concept, which "gives you the competitive edge." And the third is having a true investor's attitude toward the stock market. "If you have that attitude," says Buffett, "you start out ahead of 99 percent of all the people who are operating in the stock market—it's an enormous advantage." (OID)[1]

Developing the investor's attitude, Graham said, is a matter of being prepared, both financially and psychologically, for the market's inevitable ups and downs—not merely knowing intellectually that a downturn will happen, but having the emotional ballast needed to react appropriately when it does. In Graham's view, an investor's appropriate reaction to a downturn is the same as a business owner's response when offered an unattractive price: ignore it. "The true investor," says Graham, "scarcely ever is forced to sell his shares and at all other times is free to disregard the current price quotation."[2]

To drive home his point, Graham created an allegorical character he named "Mr. Market." The well-known story of Mr. Market is a brilliant lesson on how and why stock prices periodically depart from rationality.

Imagine that you and Mr. Market are partners in a private business. Each day, without fail, Mr. Market quotes a price at which he is willing to either buy your interest or sell you his. The business that you both own is fortunate to have stable economic characteristics, but Mr. Market's quotes are anything but. You see, Mr. Market is emotionally unstable. Some days he is cheerful and can only see brighter days ahead. On these days, he quotes a very high price for shares in your business. At other times, Mr. Market is discouraged and, seeing nothing but trouble ahead, quotes a very low price for shares in your business.

Mr. Market has another endearing characteristic, said Graham. He does not mind being snubbed. If Mr. Market's quotes are ignored, he will be back again tomorrow with a new quote. Graham warned that it is Mr. Market's pocketbook, not his wisdom, that is useful. If Mr. Market shows up in a foolish mood, you are free to ignore him or to take advantage of him, but it will be disastrous if you fall under his influence.

"The investor who permits himself to be stampeded or unduly worried by unjustified market declines in his holdings is perversely transforming his basic advantage into a basic disadvantage," said Graham. "That man would be better off if his stocks had no market quotation at all, for he would then be spared the mental anguish caused him by other persons' mistakes of judgement."[3]

Do not be stampeded by other people's misjudgment. This is the lesson that Graham preached. It is a lesson learned well by Buffett, a lesson that he in turn urges all others to embrace. It is easy to see why Warren Buffett has, on several occasions, shared the story of Mr. Market with Berkshire Hathaway shareholders. Buffett often reminds them that successful investors need good business judgment and the ability to protect themselves from the emotional whirlwind that Mr. Market unleashes, just as he reminds himself, through the story of Mr. Market, to remain insulated from the silliness of the market.

MR. MARKET, MEET CHARLIE MUNGER

More than sixty years ago, Ben Graham began writing about the irrationality that exists in the market and how investors can protect themselves from making mistakes. Yet, in all the years since, there has been little apparent change in investor behavior. Investors still act irrationally. Fear and greed still permeate the marketplace. Foolish mistakes are still the order of the day.

Evidence of skewed thinking is all around us. We see it in friends, family members, and other close associates—even, if we are honest, in ourselves. If that is too close to be comfortable, we can also find a worthwhile reality dose in research done by the professionals. In 1997, Terrance Odean, a behavioral economist at the University of California, published a study that he entitled "Why Do Investors Trade Too Much?" In the study, he summarized what he found by observing 10,000 anonymous investors.

Over a seven-year period (1987–1993), Odean tracked 97,483 trades among 10,000 randomly selected accounts of a major discount brokerage firm. First, he discovered that the accounts had an average annual turnover ratio of 78 percent, meaning that the investors sold and repurchased almost 80 percent of their portfolio each year. Next, he compared the portfolios to the market averages over four-month, one-year, and two-year periods, and, in all those periods, found two amazing results: (1) the stocks that the investors bought consistently trailed the market and (2) the stocks that they sold actually *beat* the market. Odean calculated that, over a one-year time period, the stocks that were sold outperformed the stocks that were bought by an average of three percentage points before commissions.[4]

What would inspire people to engage in such ineffective trading? Because it is not possible to ask each of the 10,000 people what was in their minds at the time, we cannot know their reasons. There may even be 10,000 different reasons. But we can deduce one thing with certainty: When it comes to money and investing, people frequently make errors in judgment.

Perhaps we have not gone far enough. Although we have been able to identify irrational behavior, we have done very little to explain exactly why investors choose the broken path. The answer can be found in a deep-rooted analysis of psychological misjudgment. To begin that investigation, we turn to Charlie Munger.

Munger has done some hard thinking about how we accumulate bits of knowledge from various fields and combine them to achieve true wisdom; remember, from Chapter 1, his notion of a latticework of models. In investing, he says, it is clear we need to understand basic accounting and finance. It is also equally important to understand statistics and probabilities. But one of the most important fields to learn from is psychology. In particular, he stresses what he calls the psychology of misjudgment.

Munger believes a key problem is that our brain takes shortcuts in analysis. We jump too easily to conclusions. We are easily misled and are prone to manipulation. "Personally, I've gotten so that I now use a kind of two-track analysis," says Charlie. "First, what are the factors that really govern the interests involved, rationally considered? And second, what are the subconscious influences where the brain at a subconscious level is automatically doing these things—which by and large are useful, but which often misfunction." (OID)[5] He uses this two-step analysis in making investment decisions: first, consider rational expectations and probabilities; then carefully evaluate the psychological factors.

A comprehensive examination of the psychology of misjudgment would overwhelm this book. However, a few important lessons in psychology warrant our attention. Ironically, the best thinking on this subject comes from the economics department at the University of Chicago—an institution known more for its Nobel prize winners who postulate the efficient market theory of rational investors. However, a former Cornell economist, Richard Thaler, joined the economics department at Chicago with the sole purpose of questioning the rational behavior of investors.

BEHAVIORAL FINANCE

Behavioral finance is an investigative study that seeks to explain market inefficiencies by using psychological theories. Observing that people often make foolish mistakes and illogical assumptions when dealing with their own financial affairs, academics, including Thaler, began to dig deeper into psychological concepts to explain the irrationalities in people's thinking. It is, as we said, a relatively new field of study, but what we are learning is fascinating, as well as eminently useful to smart investors.

Overconfidence

Several psychological studies have pointed out that errors in judgment occur because people in general are overconfident. Ask a large sample of people how many believe their skills at driving a car are above average, and an overwhelming majority will say they are excellent drivers—which leaves open the question of who the bad drivers are. Another example can be found in the medical profession. When asked, doctors believe they can diagnose pneumonia with 90 percent confidence when in fact they are right only 50 percent of the time.

Confidence per se is not a bad thing. But overconfidence is another matter, and it can be particularly damaging when we are dealing with our financial affairs. Overconfident investors not only make silly decisions for themselves but also have a powerful effect on the market as a whole.

Investors, as a rule, appear highly confident. They believe they are smarter than everyone else and can pick the winning stocks—or, at the very least, can pick the smarter money manager who in turn can beat the market. They have a tendency to overestimate their skills and their knowledge. They typically rely on information that confirms what they believe, and they disregard contrary information. In addition, their minds work to assess whatever information is readily available rather than to seek out information that is little known.

What evidence do we have of investors' overconfidence? Under the efficient market theory, investors are supposed to buy and hold securities, yet we have experienced an increased amount of trading over the past several years. Richard Thaler thinks that investors and money managers must be endowed with a belief that they have better information and therefore can profit by outsmarting other investors.

Overconfidence explains why so many money managers make wrong calls. They take too much confidence from the information they gather, and they think they are more right than they actually are. If all the players think their information is correct and they know something that others do not, the result is a great deal of trading.

"One of the hardest things to imagine is that you are not smarter than average," said Daniel Kahneman, a professor of psychology and public affairs at Princeton University.[6] But the sobering reality is that not everyone can be better than average. Overconfidence not only helps explain the excess trading but it might also explain a great deal of the volatility experienced in the market over the past few years. It is Kahneman's belief that overconfidence may very well have prompted the "irrational exuberance" warnings by Federal Reserve Chairman Alan Greenspan. Despite analysts' warnings of high valuations, investors stampeded right back into stocks.

Overreaction Bias

Thaler points to several recent studies that demonstrate how people put too much emphasis on a few chance events, thinking that they spot a trend. In particular, investors tend to fix on the most recent information they received and extrapolate from it; the last earnings report thus becomes, in their mind, a signal of future earnings. Then, believing that they see what others do not, they make quick decisions from superficial reasoning.

Overconfidence is at work here, of course; people believe they understand the data more clearly than others and interpret it better. But there is more to it. Overconfidence is exacerbated by overreaction. The behaviorists have learned that people tend to overreact to bad news and react slowly to good news. Psychologists call this *overreaction bias*. Thus, if the short-term earnings report is not good, the typical investors response is an abrupt, ill-considered overreaction, with its inevitable effect on stock prices.

Thaler describes this overemphasis on the short term as investor "myopia" (the medical term for nearsightedness), and believes most investors would be better off if they didn't receive monthly statements. In a study conducted with other behavioral economists, he proved his idea in dramatic fashion.

Thaler and his colleagues asked a group of students to divide a hypothetical portfolio between stocks and Treasury bills. But first, they sat the students in front of a computer and simulated the returns of the portfolio over a trailing twenty-five-year period. Half the students were given mountains of information, representing the market's volatile nature with ever-changing prices. The other group was given only periodic performance measured over five-year time periods. Thaler then asked each group to allocate their portfolio for the next forty years.

The group that had been bombarded by lots of information, some of which inevitably pointed to losses, allocated only 40 percent of its money to the stock market; the group that received only periodic information allocated almost 70 percent of its portfolio to stocks. Thaler, who lectures each year at the Behavioral Conference sponsored by the National Bureau of Economic Research and the John F. Kennedy School of Government at Harvard, tells the group, "My advice to you is to invest in equities and then don't open the mail."[7]

Thaler is well known for another study that demonstrates the folly of short-term decisions. He took all the stocks on the New York Stock Exchange and ranked them by performance over the preceding five years. He isolated the thirty-five best performers (those that went up in price the most) and the thirty-five worst (those that went down the most) and created hypothetical portfolios of those seventy stocks. Then he held those portfolios for a subsequent five-year period and watched as "losers" outperformed "winners" 40 percent of the time. In the real world, Thaler believes, few investors would have had the fortitude to resist overreacting at the first sign of a price downturn, and would have missed the benefit when the "losers" began to move in the other direction.[8]

These experiments neatly underscore Thaler's notion of investor myopia—shortsightedness leading to foolish decisions. Part of the reason myopia provokes such an irrational response is another bit of psychology: our innate desire to avoid loss.

Loss Aversion

According to behaviorists, the pain of a loss is far greater than the enjoyment of a gain. Many experiments, by Thaler and others, have demonstrated that people need twice as much positive to overcome a negative. On a 50/50 bet, with precisely even odds, most people will not risk anything unless the potential gain is twice as high as the potential loss.

This is known as asymmetric loss aversion: the downside has a greater impact than the upside, and it is a fundamental bit of human psychology. Applied to the stock market, it means that investors feel twice as bad about losing money as they feel good about picking a winner. This line of reasoning can be found in macroeconomic theory, which points out that during boom times, consumers typically increase their purchases by an extra three-and-a-half cents for every dollar of wealth creation. But during economic slides, consumers will actually reduce their spending by almost twice that amount (six cents) for every dollar lost in the market.

The impact of loss aversion on investment decisions is obvious and profound. We all want to believe we made good decisions. To preserve our good opinion of ourselves, we hold onto bad choices far too long, in the vague hope that things will turn around. By not selling our losers, we never have to confront our failures.

This aversion to loss makes investors unduly conservative. Participants in 401(k) plans, whose time horizon is decades, still keep as much as 30 to 40 percent of their money invested in the bond market. Why? Only a deeply felt aversion to loss would make anyone allocate funds so conservatively. But loss aversion can affect you in a more immediate way, by making you irrationally hold onto losing stocks. No one wants to admit making a mistake. But if you don't sell a mistake, you are potentially giving up a gain that you could earn by reinvesting smartly.

Mental Accounting

One final aspect of behavioral finance that deserves our attention is what psychologists have come to call mental accounting. It refers to our habit of shifting our perspective on money as surrounding circumstances change. We tend to mentally put money into different "accounts," and that determines how we think about using it.

A simple situation will illustrate. Let us imagine that you have just returned home from an evening out with your spouse. You reach for your wallet to pay the babysitter, but discover that the $20 bill you thought was there, is not. So, when you are driving the sitter home, you stop by an ATM machine, get another $20, and pay the sitter. The next day, you discover the original $20 bill in your jacket pocket.

If you're like most people, you react with something like glee. The $20 in the jacket is "found" money. Even though the first $20 and the second $20 both came from your checking account, and both represent money you worked hard for, the $20 bill you hold in your hand is money you didn't expect to have, and you feel free to spend it frivolously.

Once again, Richard Thaler provides an interesting academic experiment to demonstrate this concept. In his study, he started with two groups of people. People in the first group were given $30 in cash and told they had two choices: (1) pocket the money and walk away, or (2) gamble on a coin flip in which, if they won, they would get $9 extra, and if they lost, they would have $9 deducted. Most people (70 percent) took the gamble because they figured they would, at the very least, end up with $21 of found money. Those in the second group were offered different choices: (1) try a gamble on a coin toss: if they won they'd get $39, and if they lost they'd get $21, or (2) get an even $30 with no coin toss. More than half (57 percent) decided to take the sure money. Both groups of people stood to win the exact same amount of money with the exact same odds, but the situation was perceived differently.[9]

The implications are clear: How we decide to invest, and how we choose to manage those investments, has a great deal to do with how we think about money. For instance, mental accounting has been suggested as one further reason why people don't sell stocks that are doing badly; in their minds, the loss doesn't become real until it is acted on. Another powerful connection has to do with risk. The full impact of tolerance for risk is described later in this chapter, but, for the moment, one thing is clear: We are far more likely to take risks with found money. On a broader scale, mental accounting emphasizes one weakness of the efficient market hypothesis; it demonstrates that market values are determined not solely by the aggregated information but also by how human beings process that information.

The study of what makes us all tick is endlessly fascinating. It is particularly intriguing to me that it plays such a strong role in investing, a world that is generally presumed to be dominated by cold numbers and soulless data. When we must make investment decisions, our behavior is sometimes erratic, often contradictory, occasionally goofy. Sometimes our illogical decisions are consistently illogical, and sometimes no pattern is discernible. We make good decisions for inexplicable reasons, and bad decisions for no good reason at all.

What is particularly alarming, and what all investors need to grasp, is that they are often unaware of their bad decisions. To fully understand the markets and investing, we now know we have to understand our own irrationalities. The study of the psychology of misjudgment is every bit as valuable to an investor as the analysis of a balance sheet and income statement. You may be proficient in the art of valuing companies, but if you don't take the time to understand behavioral finance, it will be very difficult to improve your portfolio strategy and investment performance.

RISK TOLERANCE

In the same way that a strong magnet pulls together all the nearby pieces of metal, your level of risk tolerance pulls together all the elements of the psychology of finance. The psychological concepts are abstract; where they get real is in the day-to-day decisions you make about buying and selling. And the common thread in all those decisions is how you feel about risk.

In the past dozen or so years, investment professionals have devoted considerable energy to helping people assess their risk tolerance. Stockbrokers, investment counselors, and financial planners have all observed the constant changes in individual behavior. When the market rises, investors boldly add stocks to their portfolios only to readjust back to fixed-income securities when stocks swoon. The 1987 market crash is a good example. Overnight, many investors dramatically altered their portfolios, selling stocks in favor of bonds and other fixed-income securities. This flipping back and forth between being an aggressive investor and then becoming a conservative investor has prompted an investigation into risk tolerance.

At first, investment counselors thought assessing risk tolerance was simple. By using interviews and questionnaires, they could construct a risk profile for each investor. The trouble is, people's tolerance for risk is founded in emotion, and that means it changes with changing circumstances. All the principles of psychology that play into our attitudes about money also feed our response to risk. When the market declines drastically, even those with an "aggressive" profile will become very cautious. In a booming market, not only aggressive but also supposedly conservative investors add more stocks.

One other factor is at work, and it takes us back to the idea of overconfidence. In our culture, risk takers are greatly admired, and investors are subject to the very human tendency to think themselves more comfortable with risk than they actually are. They are acting out what psychologist D.G. Pruitt calls the "Walter Mitty effect."[10]

Back in the 1930s, James Thurber, one of America's greatest humorists, wrote a delightful short story called "The Secret Life of Walter Mitty," later made into a memorable movie starring Danny Kaye. Walter was a meek, mouselike fellow completely intimidated by his overbearing, sharp-tongued wife. He coped by constructing daydreams in which the mild-mannered Mitty was magically transformed into a courageous dashing hero always there to save the day. One minute he was in an agony of fear that he had forgotten his wife's errand; the next, he was a fearless bomber pilot undertaking a dangerous mission alone.

Pruitt believes investors react to the market like Walter Mitty reacted to life. When the stock market goes up, they become brave in their own eyes, and take on additional risk. But when the stock market goes down, investors scramble for the doors, fleeing and then staying out of sight.

How do we overcome the Walter Mitty effect? By finding ways to measure risk tolerance that, as much as possible, account for the richness of the phenomena. We have to look below the surface of the standard assessment questions and investigating issues driven by psychology. A few years ago, in collaboration with

Dr. Justin Green of Villanova University, I developed a risk analysis tool that focuses on personality as much as on the more obvious and direct risk factors. After studying the risk tolerance literature, both theoretical and substantive, we abstracted important demographic factors and personality orientations that, when taken together, might help people more accurately measure their risk tolerance.

We found that risk-taking propensity is connected to two demographic factors: age and gender. Older people are less willing to assume risk than younger people, and women are typically more cautious than men. There appears to be no distinction for wealth; having more money or less money does not seem to have any effect on how risk tolerant you are.

Two personality characteristics are closely related to risk tolerance: personal control orientation and achievement motivation. Personal control refers to people's sense that they can affect both their environment and decisions about their life made within this environment. People who see themselves as having this control are called "internals." In contrast, "externals" see themselves as having little control; as being like a leaf blown hither and yon by uncontrollable winds. According to our research, people who have a high propensity for taking risk were overwhelmingly classified as internals.

Achievement motivation describes the degree to which people are goal-orientated. We found that risk takers are also goal-orientated, even though a strong focus on goals may lead to sharp disappointments.[11]

Here are some questions, adapted from our risk analysis tool, that will help you think about where you stand with regard to personal control and achievement motivation.

Getting a handle on your own propensity for risk taking is not a simple matter of drawing a direct correlation between personal control and achievement motivation. To unlock the

A. Do You Control Your Destiny?

Which statement best describes your thinking?

1. [a] In the long run, people get the respect they deserve.
   [b] Unfortunately, people's worthiness often doesn't get recognized, no matter how hard they try.
2. [a] Trusting to fate has never turned out as well for me as making a decision to take a definite course of action.
   [b] I have found that what is going to happen will happen.
3. [a] What happens to me is my own doing.
   [b] Sometimes I feel that I don't have enough control over the direction my life is taking.

B. Are You Focused on Achievements?

How strongly do the following statements describe your attitudes?

1. I don't like working on a project without knowing how well I'm doing, so I make plans that allow me to measure how fast I'm proceeding toward my overall goal.
2. A key purpose in my life is to do things that have not been done before.
3. When playing a game, I am as concerned with how well I play as I am with whether I win.
4. In everything I do—work, sports, hobbies—I try to set really high standards for myself; otherwise, where's the fun of it?

(continued)

C. Is It Luck or Hard Work?

Which statement best describes your thinking?

1. [a] To make a lot of money in the stock market, what you really need is a lot of luck.

   [b] People with good skills in making decisions are the ones who make big money in the market.

2. [a] Many of the unhappy things in people's lives are partly due to bad luck.

   [b] People's misfortunes result from the mistakes they make.

3. [a] Without the right breaks, you cannot be an effective leader.

   [b] Capable people who fail to become leaders have not taken advantage of their opportunities.

4. [a] It is not always wise to plan too far ahead because many things turn out to be a matter of good or bad luck anyway.

   [b] When I make plans, I am almost certain that I can make them work.

real relationship between these personality characteristics and risk taking, you need to think about how you view the environment in which the risk is taking place.[12] That is, do you think of the stock market as (1) a game whose outcome depends on luck or (2) a contingency dilemma situation in which accurate information combined with rational choices will produce the desired results. Take a look at the next set of questions.

Now, let us consider how all these personality elements work together. For example, think about "internals," people with a strong sense of their personal ability to affect outcomes. If they believe the market is driven by chance, they will be risk averse. But if they see market results as the product of skill, "internals" have high risk-taking propensity.

According to our research, the investor who will exhibit a high degree of risk tolerance will be someone who sets goals, who believes he or she has control of the environment and can affect its outcome. This person sees the stock market as a contingency dilemma in which information, combined with rational choices, will produce winning results. Does that remind you of anyone? How would we describe Warren Buffett? How would you describe yourself?

THE PSYCHOLOGY OF FOCUS INVESTING

Everything we have learned about psychology and investing comes together in the person of Warren Buffett. He puts his faith in his own research, rather than in luck. His actions derive from carefully thought out goals, and he is not swept off course by short-term events. He understands the true elements of risk, and accepts the consequences with confidence.

Long before behavioral finance had a name, it was understood and accepted by a few renegades like Warren Buffett and Charlie Munger. Charlie points out that when he and Buffett left graduate school, they "entered the business world to find huge, predictable patterns of extreme irrationality."[13] He is not talking about predicting the timing, but rather the idea that when irrationally does occur, it leads to predictable patterns of subsequent behavior.

Buffett and Munger aside, only quite recently have the majority of investment professionals paid serious attention to the intersection of finance and psychology. For many of you, the ideas summarized in this chapter are valuable just for the sheer pleasure of learning something new. But there is much more to it.

The emotions surrounding investing are very real, in the sense that they affect people's behavior and, thus, ultimately affect market prices. You have already sensed, I am sure, two reasons why understanding the human dynamic is so valuable in your own investing:

1. You will have guidelines to help you avoid the most common mistakes.
2. You will be able to recognize other people's mistakes in time to profit from them.

All of us are vulnerable to individual errors of judgment, which can affect our personal success. When a thousand or a million people make errors of judgment, the collective impact pushes the market in a destructive direction. Then, so strong is the temptation to follow the crowd, accumulated bad judgment only compounds itself. In a turbulent sea of irrational behavior, the few who act rationally may well be the only survivors.

Successful focus investors need a certain kind of temperament. The road is always bumpy, and knowing which is the right path to take is often counterintuitive. The stock market's constant gyrations can be unsettling to investors and make them act in irrational ways. You need to be on the lookout for these emotions and be prepared to act sensibly even when instincts may strongly call for the opposite behavior. But, as we have learned, the future rewards focus investing significantly enough to warrant our strong effort.

EIGHT

The Market as a Complex Adaptive System

We've long felt that the only value of stock forecasters is to make fortune tellers look good.

—Warren Buffett

ANYONE WHO HAS observed Warren Buffett for any length of time knows that his position on forecasting is clear: Don't waste your time. Whether in regard to the economy, the market, or individual stock prices, Buffett believes firmly that forecasting has no place in investing. For over forty years, he has achieved great wealth and an unmatched performance record by simply investing in great companies while simultaneously avoiding the ruinous distractions that occur when investors become obsessed with guessing the future direction of markets.

"The fact that people will be full of greed, fear or folly is predictable," says Buffett. "The sequence, however, is not."[1]

For many Buffett followers, the idea of predicting markets is moot. They are able to push ahead with their investment approach without allowing the passing "fortune tellers" to interrupt their work. There are, however, far more investors who, despite good intentions, cannot help but be seduced by the promoter who sells clairvoyance in a bottle.

Throughout history, we humans have always been attracted to people, concepts, or systems that profess an ability to predict the future. Wizards and soothsayers, witch doctors and medicine men, palm-readers and fortune-tellers, market-timers and economic forecasters, all have held the attention of millions by simply saying, "I can tell you today what is going to happen tomorrow." Even though history is littered with the carcasses of those who were first revered but later ruined, ranks of new soothsayers come forward to take their place, knowing that they will find an eager audience.

Having access to tomorrow's paper today would impart a clear financial advantage, but I believe the urge to know the future is far more complex than mere money. I suspect that we humans have a deep psychological need to know what the future holds for us. Perhaps the idea of not knowing what lies ahead is so uncomfortable that we cannot help but be drawn to anyone or anything that can take this discomfort away. The study of this psychological weakness needs to be added to Charlie Munger's latticework of models.

Now keep in mind, Buffett does not say the future is unpredictable. After all, we do know the market will eventually reward companies able to increase their shareholders' value. But we do not know precisely when this will occur. We also can safely predict that stock prices will continue to be volatile. We just don't know if, come next year, these prices will be up or down. Benefiting from

---

The Perils of Forecasting

As one small example of how treacherous are the waters that forecasters must navigate, consider this:

Look backward at sixteen years' worth of semiannual forecasts of interest rates on thirty-year Treasury bonds (see Table 8.1). Out of the thirty-one forecasts, not only did the actual rate never match the forecast but, amazingly, the forecasters even predicted the wrong *direction* twenty-two times.

---

the Warren Buffett Way does not require us to guess correctly what the near-term future will be. It is only critical to know that we have purchased the right company. After that, we can rest assured our selection will eventually be rewarded.

If you are among those who have long ago put the issue of forecasting markets behind them, you can page forward to the concluding chapter of this book. For everyone else who is periodically tempted to follow the advice of forecasters, take a few extra minutes and read this chapter, which I hope will finally put to rest any idea that predicting the near-term future direction of the market is either necessary or worthwhile.

CLASSICAL THEORY

Classical economic theory argues that markets and economies are equilibrium systems, meaning that in their natural state they are in balance. Despite countervailing forces of supply and demand or price and quantity, the stock market and the economy

Table 8.1 Problem: Forecasting Interest Rates

	WSJ Survey of Economists (Forecast: 30 Year Treasury Bonds)						
Forecast Date	Yield Forecast (%)	Levels Actual (%)	Forecast Direction	Forecast Date	Yield Forecast (%)	Levels Actual (%)	Forecast Direction
6/82	13.05	13.92		12/89	8.12	7.97	Wrong
12/82	13.27	10.41	Right	6/90	7.62	8.40	Wrong
6/83	10.07	10.98	Wrong	12/90	8.16	8.24	Right
12/83	10.54	11.87	Wrong	6/91	7.65	8.41	Wrong
6/84	11.39	13.64	Wrong	12/91	8.22	7.39	Right
12/84	13.78	11.53	Wrong	6/92	7.30	7.78	Wrong
6/85	11.56	10.44	Wrong	12/92	7.61	7.39	Right
12/85	10.50	9.27	Wrong	6/93	7.44	6.67	Wrong
6/86	9.42	7.28	Wrong	12/93	6.84	6.34	Wrong
12/86	7.41	7.49	Right	6/94	6.26	7.61	Wrong
6/87	7.05	8.50	Wrong	12/94	7.30	7.87	Wrong
12/87	8.45	8.98	Wrong	6/95	7.94	6.62	Wrong
6/88	8.65	8.85	Right	12/95	6.60	5.94	Right
6/89	9.25	8.04	Wrong				

Observations: (1) Six-month "average" forecast of economists, (2) semiannual survey by *Wall Street Journal*, and (3) in only 9 out of 31 forecasts was the direction correct.

Source of data: *Wall Street Journal*, Revised 6/30/98.

are always able to reach a state of equilibrium. In this world, markets are efficient, mechanistic, and rational. Articulated over one hundred years ago by Alfred Marshall, this economic theory still dominates our thinking today. Michael Mauboussin, of Columbia University School of Business, explains that the Marshallian economic viewpoint "stems from the idea that economics is a science akin to Newtonian physics, with an identifiable link between cause and effect and implied predictability."[2]

Modern science, which actually began four hundred years ago, is based on the assumption that nature is governed by universal laws of cause and effect. According to Ilya Prigogine, a Nobel laureate in physics, that vision of science is based on the conviction that the future follows from the present and can be determined by a careful study of present data. This viewpoint, of course, was nothing more than a theoretical possibility. Even so, it allowed scientists to move from a world of appearances to a world of understanding.

Modern science is rooted in determinism, explains Karl Popper, a noted British philosopher of science. He says that scientific determinism is a "result of replacing the idea of God with the idea of nature and the idea of divine law by that of natural law. Nature, or perhaps the law of nature, is omnipotent as well as omniscient—it fixes everything in advance. By contrast to God, who is inscrutable and who may be known only by revelation, the laws of nature may be discovered by human reason aided by human experience. Thus if we know the laws of nature we can predict the future from the present data by purely rational methods."[3]

Isaac Newton was modern science's first determinist. His theory of gravitation established the field of mechanics, which is at the core of physics, and by doing so provided a paradigm that scientific discovery has emulated ever since. Without question, the

Newtonian model of discovery is very powerful. For centuries, it has allowed scientists to stake out new areas of knowledge.

In Isaac Newton's world, the universe is as mechanical and predictable as a clock. Over the centuries, physicists, biologists, and chemists have all established models of understanding that reflect the Newtonian vision of order. However, this prejudice in favor of the Newtonian model may have impaired our judgment. According to the British physicist James Clerk Maxwell, "Those persuaded towards determinism have always been swayed in their judgement by the fact that physicists and especially their spokesmen always focus attention upon the problems that reinforce the image of the clockwork universe."[4]

What troubles many scientists today is that the Newtonian framework does not allow us to see the world as it behaves. Newton's classical physics, which is a set of mechanical laws describing physical events, appears too rigid to describe life's richness. Make no mistake: Newton's laws are very much in effect when we must describe the trajectory of planets in orbit, but when we attempt to describe cellular reproduction, immune systems, and the behavior of human beings, the Newtonian mechanical process falls way short. It appears the classical laws of science do not provide for a better understanding of life.

For many years, a group of scientists avoided studying phenomena that did not easily conform to the Newtonian vision, and stuck closely to the view of a world in equilibrium. The geneticist Richard Lewontin "called these scientists 'Platonists' after the renowned Athenian philosopher who declared that the messy, imperfect objects we see around us are merely the reflections of perfect archetypes."[5] According to Lewontin, there is a second group of scientists who see the world as a process of change, with the material parts revolving in endless combinations. Lewontin called these scientists "Heraclitians" after the Ionian philosopher who passionately and poetically argued that the world is in a constant state of flux."[6] Heraclitus, who lived 200 years before Plato, observed that "upon those who step into the same rivers flow other and yet other waters," a statement that Plato paraphrased as "You can never step into the same river twice."[7]

"When I read what Lewontin said," says Stanford economist Brian Arthur, "it was a moment of revelation. That's when it finally became clear to me what was going on. I thought to myself, 'Yes! We're finally beginning to recover from Newton'."[8]

Brian Arthur, trained both in mathematics and economics, had struggled for years to reconcile his view of the economy with that of other economic theorists who still expounded the Marshallian view of the world. The answer to Arthur's conundrum could not be found in the ivory towers of the country's most prestigious universities or in the skyscrapers of New York, the world center of trade. The answer was found in the most unexpected place—the Sangre de Cristo Mountains of New Mexico.

THE SANTA FE INSTITUTE

In the beautiful capital city of Santa Fe, alongside old adobe houses and modern art galleries, is a spectacular hilltop structure that was once a private residence. Today, it is the home of a remarkable think tank called the Santa Fe Institute.

Perhaps it is the thin air, or the striking blue sky, or the breathtaking view of red mountains crumbling into the desert that makes people who visit Santa Fe more reflective. Whatever the reason, the Institute appears to be the perfect location for scientists who gather to theorize about theories. Scientists at the Santa Fe Institute are not doing science in typical fashion. Instead, they are openly exchanging information with one another to help construct a new way to understand life.

Established in 1984 by George Cowan, former head of research at Los Alamos Laboratory, the Santa Fe Institute is a multidisciplinary organization composed of physicists, biologists,
immunologists, psychologists, mathematicians, and economists.
Many are Nobel laureates or have achieved comparable recognition in their field; all are united in their pursuit for principles
that work across complex adaptive systems. There are no discipline boundaries. Scientists are encouraged to share their theories and ideas with people in other disciplines. At Santa Fe, you
are likely to hear a lecture on the communication patterns of
ants alongside a discussion of how economic markets spread information. Although to many the connection may appear faint,
scientists studying complexity have discovered many similarities.

In the world that surrounds us, there are many examples of
complex systems. Cells, developing embryos, brains, immune systems, central nervous systems, ecologies, and ant colonies are all
complex systems. So, too, are economies, social structures, and
political systems. The term *complexity* has no precise meaning.
Ilya Prigogine says systems are complex because a great number
of interacting elements are involved. Simple systems—an object
under the influence of gravity, or the motion of a pendulum—
contain very few moving parts. However, says Prigogine, possess-
ing a vast number of moving parts does not in itself qualify a
system as complex. A centimeter of gas may contain millions of
molecules bouncing and colliding in all possible directions, but
scientists tend to describe these systems as molecular chaos, not
complexity. Chaos, an overused term that reached the height of
popularity years ago, describes a system in which particles are
erratic and behavior is in continuous disorder.

At Santa Fe, scientists have turned their attention away from
the study of chaos and have focused instead on complex systems.
Complex systems, we have learned, exist in the boundary between
chaos and mechanical dead order. Perhaps it would be easier to

think of complex systems in terms of behavior, says Prigogine, rather than systems. It is, after all, the study of behavioral characteristics among many different complex systems that eventually may help us understand what complexity is.

In 1987, twenty invited guests met at the Santa Fe Institute to discuss the economy as a complex system. Ten theoretical economists were invited by the Nobel laureate Kenneth Arrow. Philip Anderson, a Nobel winner in physics, tapped ten scientists from the fields of physics, biology, and computer science. The meeting's intent was to stimulate new ways of thinking about the economy. In lectures and discussion groups, physicists learned about equilibrium systems and game theory, and economists attempted to understand Boolean networks and genetic algorithms. After ten days of hard work, the group adjourned, but not before identifying three important characteristics of an economy.[9]

First, an economy is a network system of many "agents" all acting in parallel. In an embryo, the agents are cells. In an economy, the agents are people. Both cells and people exist in environments that are produced by the interactions of other agents. The cells and the people continually react to what other agents in the system are doing, and thus the environment is never at rest.

Second, control of the economy is highly dispersed. There is no master cell in a developing embryo, nor is there a master controller of the economy. Yes, our economy has a Federal Reserve, and politicians can change tax laws and regulations, but the overall economy is often a result of the millions of decisions made by individuals (agents) each day. The coherent behavior within the economic system arises out of the competition or cooperation among the agents.

Third, and this is considered to be a critical characteristic of complex systems, agents in a complex system accumulate experience and adapt to a changing environment. We know that generations of organisms will rearrange their tissue through evolution;

so, too, will people adapt and learn from their experiences in the world. So important is this characteristic that complex systems are today routinely referred to as complex adaptive systems.

It is now easy to understand how characteristics of a complex adaptive system make it impossible for the economy to ever reach equilibrium. The behavior of agents, who are constantly changing, reacting, and learning, makes it certain the economy will never be at rest. Some scientists have suggested that if the economy ever reached equilibrium, it wouldn't just be stable—it would be dead.

Conventional mathematical approaches, including calculus and linear analysis, are well suited to studying unchanging particles in a fixed environment. Newton's approach still works in the repeatable mechanistic world, but it has no use to those who want to understand complex adaptive systems. To understand economies, stock markets, or other complex adaptive systems, we will need to turn to experimental mathematics and nonlinear analysis.

THE EL FAROL PROBLEM

El Farol is a bar near the Santa Fe Institute that used to feature Irish music on Thursday nights. Brian Arthur, who is now the Citigroup Professor of Economics at the Institute, was born and raised in Belfast and enjoyed going to El Farol to listen to his favorite music. But there was one slight problem. Occasionally, El Farol was packed with rambunctious drunks whom Arthur wished to avoid. The chore of having to decide, week after week, whether to go to the bar led him to formulate a mathematical theory he named the "El Farol Problem." "It has all the characteristics of a complex adaptive system," said Arthur.[10]

Suppose there are one hundred people in Santa Fe who like going to El Farol to listen to music, but none of them wants to go to the bar if it's overcrowded. Now also suppose that, each week, El Farol publishes its Thursday night attendance. Over the past ten weeks, the figures were: fifteen, eighteen, eighty-three, sixty-six, forty-five, seventy-six, sixty-seven, fifty-six, eighty-eight, and thirty-seven. Music lovers can use these past data to estimate how many people will show up at the bar next week. Some may figure that approximately the same number of people will attend this week as came last week (thirty-seven patrons). Others might take an average of the prior ten weeks (fifty-five patrons) or a shorter four-week period (sixty-two patrons).

Now let's suppose that each person who wants to go to El Farol will go if he or she estimates that fewer than sixty other people will go that evening. All of the one hundred people will decide independently, using whatever predictor has proven to be the most accurate over the past several weeks. Because each person has a different set of predictors, some people will turn up at El Farol on any given Thursday night, and others will stay home because their model predicts that more than sixty people will be at the bar. The following day, El Farol publishes the new attendance figure, and the one hundred lovers of Irish music update their models and get ready for next week's prediction.

The El Farol process, explains Arthur, can be termed an "ecology" of predictors. What he means is that, at any point, there is a subset of predictors that are deemed "alive," which means that at least one of the predictors is being used and the other predictors are "dead." Over time, some predictors will come to "life" and others will "die."

Is the El Farol problem nothing more than a theoretical proposition used to help understand the difficulties of predicting complex adaptive systems, or does it actually exist in the market today?

Each year, Merrill Lynch polls a group of institutional investors about the factor models that influence their stock selection. The poll also highlights the change in popularity of the different factor models compared to the previous year. Merrill Lynch has conducted the survey since 1989, and, during that period, investors have changed both the models they use to select stocks and the emphasis they place on different models.

The Merrill Lynch Institutional Factor Survey, containing the results of the poll, ranks the popularity of twenty-three different factor models: (1) earnings (per share) surprise, (2) return on equity, (3) earnings revisions, (4) price to cash flow ratio, (5) projected five-year profit growth, (6) debt to equity, (7) earnings (per share) momentum, (8) relative strength, (9) price to earnings ratio, (10) price to book ratio, (11) analysts' opinion changes, (12) earnings variability, (13) dividend discount model, (14) price to sales ratio, (15) neglected stocks, (16) beta, (17) earnings estimate dispersion, (18) dividend yield, (19) earnings uncertainty, (20) foreign exposure, (21) size, (22) low stock price, and (23) interest rate sensitivity. Whether we are trying to predict the future behavior of stock prices or the number of people who will attend El Farol on a Thursday night, there are countless ways to construct models.

If we isolate the top ten models used in the Merrill Lynch survey over the past nine years (see Table 8.2), we can see the El Farol problem revealing itself. Although earnings surprise is the most consistently popular model, there is variation in how other models have been put to use. For example, return on equity was the second most popular model used in 1997 but was less popular years ago. Conversely, earnings momentum, which was popular between 1989 and 1993, has fallen out of favor more recently. When Merrill Lynch began the survey in 1989, over half of the investors polled cited the importance of dividend yield in their

Table 8.2 Merrill Lynch Institutional Survey 1989–1997

Factors	1997	1996	1995	1994	1993	1992	1991	1990	1989
EPS Surprise	1	1	1	1	1	2	3	1	1
Return on Equity	2	4	4	4		1	4		
Earnings Revisions	3	2	2	2	2				
Price to Cash Flow	4	5	3	3	4	5		3	4
Projected Five Year Growth	5		5	5					
EPS Momentum		3			3	4	2	2	2
Dividend Discount Model					5				5
Price to Book						3		4	3
Debt to Equity							1		
Earnings Yield							5	5	

1–Most popular model used.
2–Second most popular model used.
3–Third most popular model used.
4–Fourth most popular model used.
5–Fifth most popular model used.

Table 8.3 Change in Factors Used: 1997 vs. 1996
Percentage Point Difference in Survey Results

Source of data: Merrill Lynch Quantitative Analysis.

174

stock selection; today, only 12 percent weight dividends in their decision process.

The Merrill Lynch survey is a good example of Arthur's ecology of predictors. In the years that were studied, we can see how some models died away and others came to life.

Table 8.2 shows a slow change in the models used over a nine-year time period. Table 8.3, which tracks a change in popularity from 1996 to 1997, displays a more dynamic shift in individual preferences. For example, debt to equity, price to cash flow, and projected five-year growth models have all shown increasing use, whereas dividend yield, earnings momentum, and earnings variability have waned in popularity.

Richard Bernstein, director of quantitative research at Merrill Lynch and overseer of the institutional survey, says: "The results are a useful gauge of which strategies have gained popularity in recent years and which ones have fallen out of favor." But the results are also troubling to Bernstein. "What I find significant in the past," he explains, "is that while many portfolio managers claim they have a disciplined approach to investing, it's clear that stock selection processes go through dramatic changes."[11]

THREE DEGREES OF SEPARATION

The problem faced by people who want to go to El Farol and by investors trying to pick stocks is that to forecast as accurately as possible means knowing full well that the actual results will be determined by the forecasts of others. It is the same problem that John Maynard Keynes recognized sixty years ago.

"Professional investment may be likened to those newspaper competitions in which the competitors have to pick out the six prettiest faces from a hundred photographs," he wrote, "the prize being awarded to the competitor whose choice most nearly corresponds to the average preferences of the competitors as a whole; so that each competitor has to pick, not those faces which he himself finds prettiest, but those which he thinks likeliest to catch the fancy of the other competitors, all of whom are looking at the problem from the same point of view."

As if trying "to guess better than the crowd how the crowd will behave" were not tricky enough, Keynes's exercise is complicated by one more variable. "It is not a case of choosing those which, to the best of one's judgement, are really the prettiest, nor even those which average opinion genuinely thinks the prettiest," said Keynes. "We have reached the third degree where we devote our intelligence to anticipating what average opinion expects the average opinion to be. And there are some, I believe, who practice the fourth, fifth, and higher degrees."[12]

This beauty contest metaphor presents the same dilemma faced by El Farol patrons and by individual investors: What counts today is not what you think is going to happen in the market or the economy but what you believe most people think about the markets. Buffett understands this well. "We have 'professional investors,' those who manage many billions, to thank for most of this turmoil," says Buffett. "Instead of focusing on what businesses will do in the years ahead, many prestigious money managers now focus on what they expect other money managers to do in the days ahead."[13]

I believe Brian Arthur's El Farol metaphor is an accurate description of what is happening in the stock market. Even though we can readily identify the market as a complex adaptive system, we are no closer to solving the problem of how to predict the behavior of such a system. But at the Santa Fe Institute, they are trying. Working with John Holland, another Institute researcher, Arthur has built an artificial stock market inside a computer populated with hundreds of investor-agents. "These little guys get smart by learning which one of their strategies works best," explains Arthur. "As they learn, they're changing around strategies, which changes the nature of the market."[14]

The study of human behavior does not require us to clone an entire human being. It is possible today, using high-powered computers, to replicate the behavior of individuals by importing digital agents with a handful of simple rules. Still, we have not developed the mathematical structures that will solve the El Farol problem. "Mathematically, we are stuck," says John Casti, mathematician, author, and a Fellow at the Institute. "This is symptomatic of the whole field. We have no good mathematical framework within which to probe the properties of complex adaptive systems."[15]

Casti believes that today we face the same problems as did the seventeenth-century gamblers trying to separate the stakes of a game that was stopped prematurely. Pascal and Fermat saw the problem and developed the mathematical structure that is now called probability theory. "Complex system theory," says Casti, "still awaits its Pascal and Fermat."[16]

INVESTING IN A COMPLEX WORLD

Benjamin Graham had an interdisciplinary approach to thinking about the world in general, and investing in particular. Those who have studied Graham know he was not only a great financial thinker but also one who appreciated philosophy and the classics. Although he is best known for his analysis of common stock investing, Graham's contributions included work in the study of currencies and commodities. *Storage and Stability* and *World Commodities and World Currencies* demonstrated Graham's worldly view. "Ben Graham was an incredible teacher and a very well-rounded individual," said Michael Mauboussin, who today teaches the Security Analysis class that Graham originated. "His interdisciplinarian appreciation of the world made the context of his course Security Analysis much greater."[17]

At Columbia University, Professor Mauboussin is not only teaching basic finance models but is also studying other models from other disciplines. By doing so, he hopes to enlighten students on how multidisciplinary models might apply in the investing world. "As time has gone on, because of the backdrop of the world economy and the social economic situations, our mental models have to evolve," explains Mauboussin. Thirty years ago, technology was not represented in any meaningful way in our investment thinking. Today, technology has become very prominent, and that, according to Mauboussin, has required us to evolve our mental models to better understand the world around us. "On the Shoulders of Giants: Mental Models for the New Millenium"[18] was Mauboussin's effort to help students separate the older equilibrium models from the more dynamic models, in an attempt to interface with how the world actually works. "My gut feeling is that complex adaptive systems is a very powerful way of understanding how capital markets operate," says Mauboussin. "As complex adaptive systems become better understood, I believe investors will have much better descriptions of how markets actually work."[19]

It is important to appreciate the difference between analyzing how a market works and trying to predict the market. We are coming closer to understanding the behavior of markets, but we have not yet acquired any predictive powers. The lesson of complex adaptive systems is that the market is ever changing and stubbornly defies prediction.

"We believe the economy's too complicated to forecast," says Legg Mason's Bill Miller. "You'll never add any value to a portfolio by conforming it to an economic or market forecast."[20] Miller, like Buffett, never lets forecasting interfere with his decision making about individual stocks, but neither has it prevented him from studying the behavior of markets. "We spend a lot of time trying to understand the best academic thinking on markets," says Miller. "Part of what has helped us is understanding complex adaptive systems as they relate to markets and behavioral finance."[21]

Bill Miller first learned about the Santa Fe Institute in an article on chaos theory by James Gleick, a science writer for the *New York Times*. Miller began to wonder whether the study of complex systems would give him insight about investing. In 1991, his work brought him into contact with Citicorp President John Reed, who provided the seed funding for the Institute's Economics Program.

The problem with investing, explains Miller, is that everyone in the investment business is moving in the same circles, reading the same research reports and books. Investors are all getting the same information from the same sources. At the Santa Fe Institute, Miller reads books and research papers from scientists who are studying complex adaptive systems. "Their research provides insights for practical businesspeople like myself," says Miller. "It is not the job of any researcher to help us beat the market, but they are happy to talk about their work."[22]

Today, Miller, who serves on the Institute's board of trustees, believes that his experience in Santa Fe has opened new arenas of thought for him. "The economy," he says, "like other complex adaptive systems under investigation at the Institute, is a multiagent environment with many local rules and feedback loops. Where Santa Fe really applies to what we do is when we see how these system components and forecasting agents are 'cognized' by the researchers at the Institute. It has helped us let go of simple models and think more creatively about the market's complexity."[23]

For example, the economy is often viewed as a jungle habitat where competitors fiercely fight with each other for market survival. However, studies by ecologists revealed that there are many examples of peaceful coexistence among species normally thought to be enemies. In a book on complex systems written at the Institute, ecologists noted that two of birds, thought to compete for the same food supply, were inhabiting the same tree. One species kept to the higher branches while the other nestled on the lower branches.

Reading this, Miller began to think about the computer industry and the dogfight that existed between Dell and Compaq. "Compaq isn't necessarily in direct competition with Dell Computer," thought Miller. "The competition dynamics are much more complicated than many people realize. Actually, both companies have their own niche in the marketplace."[24]

Miller also believes investors need to think differently about today's stock market. Pointing out that the S&P 500 includes a lot more technology companies with very different financial characteristics, the market today is very different from its composition in the 1960s (see Table 8.4) In 1964, technology companies represented only 5.5 percent of the weight of the S&P 500, and basic materials represented 16.5 percent. Today, these two industry groups have almost swapped places. Basic materials has shrunk to 6.9 percent, and technology has jumped to 12.0 percent and is still growing. There are other important differences. In the 1960s, utilities and oil represented 37 percent of the index. Today, these two groups weigh in at 19 percent. Finance and health care, once insignificant to the index, today constitute a quarter of it.

"Most investors only use historical valuation methodologies or models to determine when stocks are cheap or expensive," says Bill Miller. "But the problem with historical valuation

Table 8.4   The S&P 500: This Is Not Your Father's Index

Sector	Capitalization Weight	
	1964 (%)	1996 (%)
Finance	2.0	14.6
Health	2.3	10.7
Consumer Nondurables	9.0	12.8
Consumer Services	6.3	9.7
Consumer Durables	10.8	2.7
Energy	17.8	8.9
Transportation	2.6	1.6
Technology	5.5	12.0
Basic Materials	16.5	6.9
Capital Goods	8.0	9.9
Utilities	19.2	10.2
Grand Total	100.0	100.0

methodologies is that they are context-dependent. That is to say, the measurements arose in the context of a particular economic environment, particular returns on capital, particular business situations and strategies."[25] In other words, historical models work as long as the context in which the companies and industries are operating is similar to the context in which the valuation methodologies were first established. What we see today, compared to the 1960s, is an environment that is massively different for individual companies and ultimately for the index to which many investors compare them.

The stock market reflects the cumulative behavior of billions of decisions made by millions of investors, traders, and speculators. Each of these decisions is independent from all others. Each person has only a partial view of the market but acts on that information. When all these agents interact, a market is formed.

But in a complex adaptive system, we can't predict what is going to happen by simply investigating the individual actors. In a complex adaptive system, the whole is greater than the sum of the parts.

Sometimes, the behavior of the parts creates a trend. However, because each agent has only limited knowledge, everyone perceives a trend but no one has any idea what caused it. Because all the agents in the market are reacting to one another, a price trend develops. It is this trend that leads some people to venture predictions. For example, a stock will fall within a trading range that entices traders into repeated patterns of buying and selling. But, at some point, explains Miller, small unrecognized changes in behavior slowly creep into the market. Eventually, a critical point is reached. Professor Mauboussin likens the changes in markets to a sand pile that is formed by a slow but steady pouring of sand. "Each grain," explains Mauboussin, "is like an individual agent. Insignificant in itself, it joins with other grains to produce cumulative effects. Once the pile grows past some critical point, the system falls out of balance."[26] The result is an avalanche.

Minute changes are always creeping into the market. What frightens investors, explains Miller, "is the trend breaks down without forewarning of a simple outside event. Investors get caught short because none of these inputs is big enough to draw attention."[27]

Investors are always betting that a stock, or the market as a whole, regresses to the mean—that it follows some predictable pattern. But the mean is not stable. It is always shifting and changing, based on the unpredictable decisions of millions of investors who themselves are adjusting to other decisions. Miller cautions that basing decisions on patterns carries much risk. "You think of the market as a simple linear situation. But the market is nonlinear, complex, adaptive. So your system works until it suddenly just stops working."[28]

PATTERN RECOGNITION

"Something about the mind, wired to find patterns both real and imaginary, rebels at the notion of fundamental disorder."[29] Those words, written by George Johnson in his readable book *Fire in the Mind,* reveal the dilemma that all investors face. The mind craves patterns, argues Johnson; patterns suggest order, which allows us to plan and make use of our resources. But this natural drive for order bounces up against its limits when we study the market. "If you have a truly complex system," says Brian Arthur, "then the exact patterns are not repeatable."[30]

If the Santa Fe Institute studies enough complex systems, it may allow us to observe, by metaphor, the behavior of one particular complex system. Until then, we are destined to live with a market that shows only limited patterns of behavior constantly interrupted by unexpected and sometimes violent changes. Like it or not, we live in an ever-changing world. Like a kaleidoscope, patterns in this world change with some apparent order but never repeat in the exact sequence. The patterns are always new and different.

How do investors maneuver in a world that lacks pattern recognition? By looking in the right place at the right level. Although the economy and the market as a whole are too complex and too large to be predictable, there are patterns at the company level that we can recognize. Inside each company, there are company patterns, management patterns, and financial patterns.

If you study those patterns, in most cases you can make a reasonable prediction about the future of that company. Those are the patterns that Warren Buffett focuses on, not the unpredictable behavioral patterns of million of investors. "I have always found it easier to evaluate weights dictated by fundamentals than votes dictated by psychology," he said.[31]

"We will continue to ignore political and economic forecasts, which are an expensive distraction for many investors and businessmen," says Buffett. "Thirty years ago, no one could have foreseen the huge expansion of the Vietnam War, wage and price controls, two oil shocks, the resignation of a president, the dissolution of the Soviet Union, a one-day drop in the Dow of 508 points, or Treasury bill yields fluctuating between 2.8 percent and 17.4 percent."[32]

Not knowing ahead of time when these events would occur did not prevent Buffett from achieving his investment performance. "None of these blockbuster events made the slightest dent in Ben Graham's investment principles," said Buffett. "Nor did they render unsound the negotiated purchases of fine businesses at sensible prices. Imagine the cost to us, if we had let a fear of unknowns cause us to defer or alter the deployment of capital."[33]

Patterns of speech follow patterns of thought. If investors perceive a pattern, no matter how flawed the recognition, they will act on the pattern recognition. The benefit of the Santa Fe Institute is that it helps you understand what the markets are *not*. Once you understand that the market is a complex adaptive system, you freely put to rest any notion of predictability. You also understand that the market will reach critical points of boom and bust.

"A different set of major shocks is sure to occur in the next thirty years," explains Buffett. "We will neither try to predict these nor profit from them. If we can identify businesses that are similar to those we have purchased in the past, external surprises will have little effect on our long-term results."[34]

So the next time you are lulled into believing you have finally identified a repeatable pattern primed for profit, remember the scientists working each day at the Santa Fe Institute. And the next time you are shocked frozen by the market's unpredictability, remember what Buffett says. "Face up to two unpleasant facts: the future is never clear and you pay a very high price in the stock market for a cheery consensus. Uncertainty is the friend of the buyer of long-term values."[35]

NINE

Where Are the .400 Hitters?

The first rule of baseball is, get a good ball to hit.
—Rogers Hornsby

IN 1996, Stephen Jay Gould, the noted biologist, prolific writer, and lifelong Yankees fan, published *Full House: The Spread of Excellence from Plato to Darwin*. Gould is fascinated by the complex nature of life, and he studies intensely the variations of different systems. In this illuminating book, he talks about, among other things, the death of .400 hitting in major league baseball.

The record books say that between 1901 and 1930, a span of thirty years, there were nine seasons when at least one player achieved a batting average better than .400. But in the sixty-eight years that followed, only one player ever reached that milestone: Ted Williams hit .406 in 1941.

From those statistics, we might conclude that batting skills, over time, have deteriorated. But Gould wants us to consider the ease with which statistics can be misread. He believes another force is at work. Hitting is not getting worse but, overall, the defense is getting better. The pitching is more sophisticated, the fielding skills are better, and the teams' ability to develop a full defense against strong hitting is much advanced. Gould the scientist explains, "As play improves and the bell curve marches towards the right wall, variation must shrink at the right tail. [And] .400 hitting disappears as a consequence of increasing excellence in play."[1]

Peter L. Bernstein, founding editor of the *Journal of Portfolio Management* and author of two outstanding works on finance— *Capital Ideas: The Improbable Origins of Modern Wall Street* and *Against the Gods: The Remarkable Story of Risk*—takes Gould's thesis on .400 hitting and applies it to the business of portfolio management. "The performance data for equity portfolio managers," he says, "reveal patterns that are astonishingly similar to what has happened in baseball."[2] Bernstein reasons that a lack of above-average performance by professional money managers is a result of the ever-increasing level of investment management education and knowledge. As more and more people become more and more skilled at investing, the odds of a breakout performance by a few superstars diminish.

It is an intriguing analogy. Following this argument to the end, one could conclude that heavy hitters like Warren Buffett will gradually be displaced completely by an efficient market of well-informed, intelligent investors. Indeed, Bernstein points out that Berkshire Hathaway's record, when compared against the S&P 500, was better in the 1960s and 1970s than in the 1980s and 1990s. However, I would argue that, considering that the stock market is more competitive today and that Berkshire's enlarged capital base becomes a relative handicap in this kind of comparison, Warren Buffett still qualifies as a .400 hitter.

BECOMING A .400 HITTER

In Bernstein's article, which he titled "Where, Oh Where Are the .400 Hitters of Yesteryear?" he willingly left the back door unlocked in his performance hypothesis. He wrote that, to become a .400 hitter, the portfolio manager must be willing "to make the kinds of concentrated bets that are essential if the aim is to provide high excess returns."[3] Never mind that Bernstein believes the risk of tracking error and high standard deviation would dissuade any portfolio manager from taking on a focus portfolio. The fact still remains: A focus portfolio stands the best chance of beating a market rate of return.

Not surprising, if we open Bernstein's back door and look out, whom do we see? John Maynard Keynes, Phil Fisher, Warren Buffett, Charlie Munger, Lou Simpson, and Bill Ruane. And, just as a young rookie might have intently watched Ted Williams, we can learn a great deal by studying the batting stance and swing

---

Becoming a Portfolio Manager Who Hits .400

- Think of stocks as businesses.
- Increase the size of your investment.
- Reduce portfolio turnover.
- Develop alternative performance benchmarks.
- Learn to think in probabilities.
- Recognize the psychology of misjudgment.
- Ignore market forecasts.
- Wait for the fat pitch.

---

of these .400 hitters. As Buffett once said, "The key to life is to figure out who to be the batboy for."[4]

Think of Stocks as Businesses

"In our view," says Buffett, "investment students need only two well-taught courses—How to Value a Business, and How to Think About Market Prices."[5]

The necessary first step for anyone who wants to emulate Warren Buffett's approach is to think about stocks first and foremost as businesses. "Whenever Charlie and I buy common stocks for Berkshire, we approach the transaction as if we were buying into a private business. We look at the economic prospects of the business, the people in charge of running it, and the price we must pay."[6] The specifics of what he looks for are presented in the Warren Buffett Way investment tenets, which you will find summarized in Chapter 1.

"Your goal as an investor should be simply to purchase, at a rational price, a part interest in an easily understandable business whose earnings are virtually certain to be materially higher, five, ten, and twenty years from now," explains Buffett. "Over time, you will find only a few companies that meet these standards—so when you see one that qualifies, you should buy a meaningful amount of stock."[7]

Increase the Size of Your Investment

"I wouldn't want to buy anything where I wouldn't want to put 10 percent of my net worth into it," confesses Buffett. "If I don't want to put that into it, then it just isn't much of an idea." (OID)[8]

How many stocks should an investor own? Buffett would tell you it depends on your investment approach. If you have the ability to analyze and value businesses, then you are not likely to need many stocks. Buffett believes that the only investors who need wide diversification are those who do not understand what they are doing.

As a buyer of businesses, there is no law that requires you to own something from every major industry. And you are not required to include forty, fifty, or a hundred stocks in your portfolio to achieve adequate diversification. If a business owner would be comfortable owning ten companies, why, asks Buffett, should it be any different for an owner of common stocks?

Wide diversification is a two-edged sword. If an investor has no skills at analyzing businesses, then a broadly diversified portfolio like an index fund is the right course of action. However, we have also learned that overdiversification actually hampers the investment results of a bright stock picker by limiting the size of each individual common stock position. Even the high priests of modern finance have discovered that, on average, "85 percent of the available diversification is achieved with a fifteen-stock portfolio and increases to 95 percent with a thirty-stock portfolio."[9] Buffett asks us to consider: If the best business you own presents the least financial risk and has the most favorable long-term prospects, why would you put money into your twentieth favorite business rather than add money to the top choices?

Reduce Portfolio Turnover

It is wrong to assume that constant buying and selling will help you make progress in your portfolio. We already know that portfolio turnover creates transactions costs, which reduce your total return. For taxable investments, the effects of high turnover are far more damaging. Each time a stock is sold, assuming the transaction results in a profit, you must forgo part of the reward in the form of taxes. Remember, the unrealized capital gain in your portfolio is yours to keep as long as you own the stock. By holding on to the gain, assuming the investment tenets behind owning the company have not changed, you are able to compound your net worth more forcefully.

Treat your portfolio as if you were the chief executive officer of a holding company. "A parent company," says Buffett, "that owns a subsidiary with superb long-term economics will not sell the company's 'crown jewel.' Yet this same CEO will impulsively sell stocks in his personal portfolio with little more logic than 'You can't go broke taking a profit.' In our view," explains Buffett, "what makes sense in business also makes sense in stocks: An investor should ordinarily hold a small piece of an outstanding business with the same tenacity that an owner would exhibit if he owned all of that business."[10]

Develop Alternative Performance Benchmarks

The focus investing approach is an economic-based rather than a price-based model. In an economic-based model, concentrating the portfolio around a few select stocks is emphasized because it allows you to better understand and monitor the businesses you own. In an economic-based model, it is understood that owning fewer stocks, as opposed to more, works to reduce the overall economic risk of the portfolio. Volatility, in an economic-based model, is good because it gives you an opportunity to buy more shares of great businesses at attractive prices. Conversely, in a price-based model, diversification is broad, ownership is detached, and volatility is perceived negatively.

In an economic-based model, you are comforted in the knowledge that future share prices of stocks correlate strongly to the underlying economics of the business. If the economics of the business improve, the share price will likely rise; if the economics of the business deteriorate, the future price of your business can be expected to fall.

In this framework, you have a winner's advantage, a method with a high probability of success. The opposite approach—trying to outguess what short-term prices will be—is a loser's game. However, just because an economic-based model does not rely on short-term price changes as measures of progress, this does not mean that focus investors are left without a way to gauge their performance. It only means they need to call on a different measuring stick.

Focus investors can measure the progress of their portfolio by calculating the look-through earnings, just as Buffett does. To calculate the total earning power of your companies, multiply the earnings per share by the number of shares you own. The goal of the business owner, Buffett explains, is to create a portfolio of companies that, in ten years, will produce the highest level of look-through earnings.

Learn to Think in Probabilities

We already know that Warren Buffett is passionate about the game of bridge. You will probably not be surprised that he and Charlie Munger see many parallels between the card game and investing. "Our approach to investing," says Charlie, "is the same way you would work out a bridge problem: by evaluating the real probabilities." (OID)[11]

Buffett's favorite book on the game is called *Why You Lose at Bridge,* by S.J. Simon. It contains several insights that focus investors should take note of. According to Simon, "The card player who takes the trouble to be aware of the mathematical principles involved in his game is the rare exception—and usually a professional at that. It is not his superior skill that brings him the bulk of his profits—it is his superior mathematical awareness."[12]

Any game of cards, whether the game is bridge, poker, or blackjack, is mainly mathematical. So too is investing, but the mathematics of investing, remember, are not out of reach. The algebra involved in a Bayesian inference is high school level. In investing, of course, the exercise of pure math often has to be supplemented with subjective probability analysis, and those skills come from your business experience. Buffett has said, on several occasions, that he is a better investor because he is a businessperson and a better businessperson because he is an investor.

As you spend more time thinking about stocks as businesses, reading annual reports and trade magazines, and investigating economics as opposed to stock prices, the notion of probability will come more naturally. You will be surprised at how quickly you begin to see the business patterns that exist beneath the daily price changes. "You do see repetition of certain business patterns and business behavior," Buffett points out. "And Wall Street tends to ignore those, incidentally." (OID)[13]

If you become the sort of investor who focuses on the underlying business patterns, you will find that you are more easily able to think in probabilities, and that will be a tremendous competitive advantage. After all, says Simon, what prevents good bridge players from becoming great bridge players is "mathematical apathy."

Recognize the Psychology of Misjudgment

Blaise Pascal, one of the fathers of probability theory, said, "The mind of man at one and the same time is both the glory and the shame of the universe." (OID)[14] Charlie Munger has done a great service to investors by outlining his thoughts on psychology and investing. He says, "The mind of man has both enormous power as well as standard misfunctions that often cause it to reach wrong conclusions." (OID)[15]

The psychology involved in investing is all-important. We can get the economics right and get the probabilities right, but if we allow our emotions to override our good judgment, there will be no benefit to the focus investment approach—or any other investment approach, for that matter.

It is important to remember that the focus investment approach is not for everyone. It is a unique style that is often at odds with how the majority of people think about investing. "Each person," says Charlie, "has to play the game given his marginal utility considerations and in a way that takes into account his own psychology." According to Charlie, "If losses are going to make you miserable—and some losses are inevitable—you might be wise to utilize a very conservative pattern of investment and saving all your life." (OID)[16]

Buffett would concur. As long as you have a long-term investment horizon, the risk of focus investing, says Buffett, "becomes the risk of you yourself—of whether you're able to retain your belief in the real fundamentals of the business and not get too concerned about the stock market." (OID)[17]

Ignore Market Forecasts

At the end of 1997, who would have guessed that Japan, the world's second largest economy, would sink into the worst recession–depression in the post-World War II era? Who could have predicted that Russia would default on its debt payments, that the Southeast Asian markets would implode, and that, in a span of six weeks, the Dow Jones Industrial Average would plunge 1,800 points only to regain new highs three short months later?

The answer is: No one predicted these results, and if anyone claims that they did, the probabilities of their making a second accurate prediction are no greater than the odds on a coin toss. The stock market (and the world economy of which it is a part) is a complex adaptive system that is in a perpetual state of evolution. Simple predictive models may, for a short while, appear to be robust, but they will ultimately fail. Embracing them can be enticing, but it is foolhardy.

Buffett says that the stock market is frequently efficient. When it is efficient, information randomly becomes available in the marketplace, and participants quickly work to set prices. But note—he does not say the market is *always* efficient. From time to time, the prices set by market participants do not accurately reflect a company's intrinsic value. Stock prices disengage from the intrinsic value of a business for various reasons, including psychological overreaction as well as economic misjudgment. Focus investors are perfectly positioned to take advantage of this mispricing. But, to the degree they incorporate macroeconomic or stock market predictions inside their model, focus investors will diminish their competitive advantage.

Wait for the Fat Pitch

Ty Cobb once said, "Ted Williams sees more of the ball than any man alive—but he demands a perfect pitch." That intense discipline may explain why Williams is the only .400 hitter in the past seven decades. Warren Buffett is a great admirer of Ted Williams and, on several occasions, has shared Williams's disciplined approach with Berkshire's shareholders. In *The Science of Hitting*, Williams explained his technique. He divided the strike zone into seventy-seven cells, each representing the size of a baseball. Now, said Buffett, "Swinging only at balls in his 'best' cell,

Williams knew, would allow him to hit .400; reaching for the balls in his 'worst' spot, the low outside corner of the strike zone, would reduce him to .230."[18]

The investment analogy of Williams's hitting advice is obvious. For Buffett, investing is a series of "business" pitches, and, to achieve above-average performance, he must wait until a business comes across the strike zone in the "best" cell. Buffett believes investors too often swing at bad pitches, and their performance suffers. Perhaps it is not that investors are unable to recognize a good pitch—a good business—when they see one; maybe the difficulty lies in the fact that investors can't resist swinging the bat.

How do we overcome this dilemma? Warren Buffett recommends that investors act as if they owned a "lifetime decision card" with only twenty punches on it. Throughout your life, you get to make only twenty investment choices. Each time you swing the bat, your card is punched and you have one fewer investment available for the remainder of your life. This would force you to look only for the best investment opportunities.

Don't be tempted to swing at the pitches that are low and outside. Williams, waiting for his best pitch, took the risk of striking out. In that regard, investors have it easier, Buffett says. Unlike Williams, "We can't be called out if we resist three pitches that are barely in the strike zone."[19]

THE RESPONSIBILITY OF FOCUS INVESTORS: FAIR WARNING LABEL

Before you put this book down, it is critically important that you think seriously about what is said next. It has been suggested that *The Warren Buffett Way* and *The Warren Buffett Portfolio,* taken together, give investors something like an owner's manual to a

Ferrari. But if you took the wheel of a high-performance sports car capable of speeds approaching 200 miles per hour, you would have a responsibility to drive it safely. You would be wise to not only read the manual but follow closely the boldface warnings. Similarly, if you are ready to strap on a focus portfolio, I have a few warnings for you:

- Do not approach the market unless you are willing to think about stocks, first and always, as part ownership interests in a business.
- Be prepared to diligently study the businesses you own, as well as the companies you compete against, with the idea that no one will know more about your business or industry than you do.
- Do not even start a focus portfolio unless you are willing to invest for a minimum of five years. Longer time horizons will make for safer rides.
- Never leverage your focus portfolio. An unleveraged focus portfolio will help you reach your goals fast enough. Remember, an unexpected margin call on your capital will likely wreck a well-tuned portfolio.
- Accept the need to acquire the right temperament and personality to drive a focus portfolio.

As a focus investor, your goal is to reach a level of understanding about your business that is unmatched on Wall Street. You may protest that this is unrealistic, but, considering what Wall Street promotes, it may not be as hard as you think. If you are willing to work hard at studying businesses, you will likely get to know more about the company you own than the average investor, and that is all you need to gain a competitive advantage.

Buffett claims that his investment approach is not beyond the comprehension of the serious investor. I agree. You do not have to be an MBA-level authority on business valuation to profit from the focus approach. However, it does require you to commit your time to studying the process. As Buffett says, "Investing is easier than you think, but harder than it looks."[20] Successful investing does not require you to learn highbrow mathematics stuffed with Greek symbols. You do not have to learn to decipher derivatives and international currency fluctuations. You do not need a deep understanding of Federal Reserve policy, and you certainly do not need to follow the utterances *du jour* of the market forecasters.

Some investors would rather chatter about "what the market is doing" than bother to read an annual report. But, believe me, a "cocktail conversation" about the future direction of markets and interest rates will be far less profitable than spending thirty minutes reading the latest communication provided by the company you own.

WHY HAS WALL STREET IGNORED FOCUS INVESTING?

Amazingly, in an industry noteworthy for copying success, Wall Street has somehow managed to disregard focus investing up to now, even though its practitioners have enjoyed phenomenal results. "That practice of ours [concentrated portfolios], which is so simple, is not widely copied," Charlie Munger said. "I do not know why not. It's copied among Berkshire shareholders. All of you [shareholders] have learned it. But it's not the standard in investment management—even at great universities and other intellectual institutions. And that is a very interesting question: If we're right, why are so many eminent places wrong?" (OID)[21]

Charlie has hit upon a fundamental question: Why do people reject ideas? Particularly, we should ask, why are ideas rejected when they appear to work with great success? The person best qualified to answer this question was Thomas Kuhn.

Kuhn, who died in 1996, was a physicist turned philosopher. His 1962 masterpiece, *The Structure of Scientific Revolutions,* is considered one of the most, if not *the* most, influential philosophical works of the latter half of the twentieth century. The book, which has sold over a million copies, introduced the concept of paradigms and the now-familiar phrase "paradigm shifts."

It was Kuhn's contention that progress in science does not always occur smoothly. Although we might think that scientific discovery is a process of adding intellectual bricks to an already sturdy edifice, Kuhn showed that scientific progress sometimes occurs by crisis—first by tearing down the intellectual fabric of the prevailing model or paradigm, and then by reconstructing a brand-new model.

History appears to validate Kuhn's theory. The Copernican revolution replaced the idea of earth's centrality, and Einstein's general theory of relativity unseated Euclidean geometry. In each case, before there was a paradigm shift, explained Kuhn, there was first a crisis period. Some people believe that the current intellectual tug-of-war between broadly diversified portfolios and focus portfolios is such a crisis.

According to Kuhn, the first step in a paradigm shift occurs when an anomaly is introduced. "I've always found the word 'anomaly' interesting," said Buffett, "because Columbus was an anomaly, I suppose—at least for a while. What it means is something the academicians can't explain. And rather than reexamine their theories, they simply discard any evidence of that sort as anomalous." (OID)[22]

For years, academicians attempted to explain Buffett as an anomaly, or what statisticians call a five-sigma event. In their view, Buffett was so unusual that his success would occur only rarely and could be duplicated only by chance. Some economists used the classic orangutan analogy: If you put enough orangutans in a room, statistically one of them has to be a Buffett phenomenon. But if that is so, how are we to explain the success of John Maynard Keynes, Phil Fisher, Charlie Munger, Lou Simpson, and Bill Ruane?

One of the principal reasons why new paradigms begin to take shape is that the older paradigms begin to break down. When that happens, often the proponents of the old paradigm quickly slap on mending tape in an all-out attempt to save their model. When Ptolemy's paradigm could no longer explain the celestial shifts, astronomers simply added rings to the model in an attempt to explain what was happening in the sky. Ptolemy wasn't wrong, they insisted; the model simply needed to be refined.

You might think that, in today's world, scientists readily accept new and even contradictory information and then work collegially to construct a new paradigm. Nothing could be further from the truth, said Kuhn. "Though they [the proponents of the current paradigm] may begin to lose faith and then consider alternatives, they do not renounce the paradigm that has led them into crisis."[23] Having invested so deeply in an education and business that preach the current model, the idea of accepting a paradigm shift is an intellectual, emotional, and financial risk not worth taking.

Historically, when paradigm shifts do occur, they stretch over many decades and involve multiple generations, which allows ample time to educate new proponents. When it can no longer be denied that the old paradigm has gone massively astray, there appears on the horizon an unstoppable force of new paradigm proponents. Until the shift is completed, the biggest challenge is how proponents of the new model can survive in a world hostile to their success.

Kuhn told us that surviving a paradigm crisis requires defiance and faith. I suggest that the Superinvestors of Buffettville demonstrate both, and, considering their level of success, the rest of us would do well to follow their lead.

INVESTMENT VERSUS SPECULATION

The great financial thinkers, including John Maynard Keynes, Ben Graham, and Warren Buffett, have all taken a turn at explaining the differences between investment and speculation. According to Keynes, "Investment is an activity of forecasting the yield on assets over the life of the asset; . . . speculation is the activity of forecasting the psychology of the market."[24] For Graham, "An investment operation is one which, upon thorough analysis, promises safety of principal and a satisfactory return. Operations not meeting this requirement are speculative."[25] Buffett believes: "If you're an investor, you're looking at what the asset—in our case, businesses—will do. If you're a speculator, you're primarily forecasting on what the price will do independent of the business." (OID)[26]

Generally, they all agree that speculators are obsessed with guessing future prices while investors focus on the underlying asset, knowing that future prices are tied closely to the economic performance of the asset. If they are correct, it would appear that much of the activity that dominates the financial markets today is speculation, not investing.

It is an old but persistent debate, with passionate proponents on both sides. Shortly before his death, Ben Graham was interviewed at length by Charles Ellis. Ellis, who is a partner with Greenwich Partners and author of *Winning the Loser's Game,* conducted the interview in 1976 for the *Financial Analysts Journal.* In that interview, Ellis recalled an earlier discussion with Graham about the investment-versus-speculation debate. According to Ellis, it was not so much the concept of speculation per se that bothered Graham. Speculators, explained Graham, had always been a part of the stock market. What troubled Graham deeply was his belief that investors had unknowingly acquired speculative habits.

Perhaps we have been looking at this question the wrong way. Instead of getting into a shouting contest about what is investment and what is speculation, maybe we should concern ourselves more with the element of knowledge.[27] I would argue that as you gain more understanding about how businesses work and stock prices behave; as you begin to understand that focus portfolios, as opposed to broadly diversified portfolios, give the best chance of outperforming index funds; as you begin to appreciate that high-turnover portfolios increase your investment cost while low-turnover portfolios increase your potential return, and that chasing stock prices is a fool's game, then you begin to lay the bricks of knowledge that drive you toward an investment approach and away from speculation.

We can say with certainty that knowledge works to increase our investment return (see Figure 9.1) and reduces our overall risk (see Figure 9.2). I believe we can also make the case that knowledge is what defines the difference between investment and speculation (see Figure 9.3). In the end, the greater your level of knowledge, the less likely that pure speculation will dominate your thinking and your actions.

The talented financial writer Ron Chernow claims that "financial systems reflect the values of societies."[28] I believe that is largely true. From time to time, we seem to misplace our values, and then our markets succumb to speculative forces. Soon, we

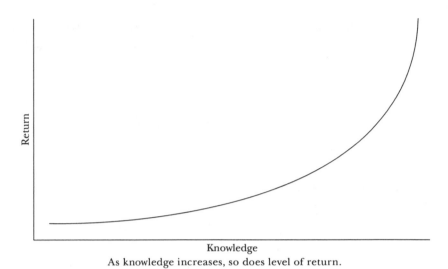

Knowledge
As knowledge increases, so does level of return.

Figure 9.1   The relationship between knowledge and financial return.

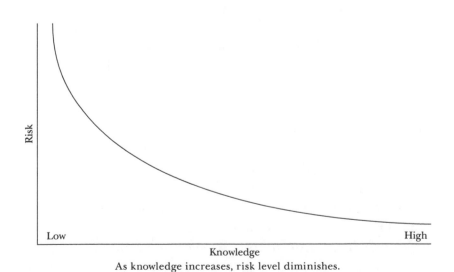

Knowledge
As knowledge increases, risk level diminishes.

Figure 9.2   The relationship between knowledge and risk.

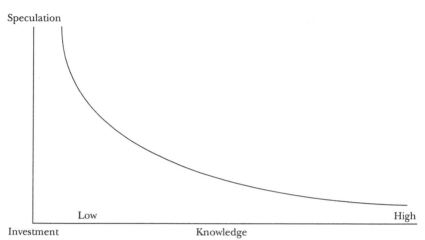

Speculation

Low   High

Investment   Knowledge

As knowledge increases, the practice of investment relative to speculation increases.

Figure 9.3 The relationship between knowledge and investment/speculation.

right ourselves and continue on with our financial walk, only to trip again and fall back into destructive habits. One way to stop the vicious cycle is to educate ourselves about what works and what does not.

LEARNING FROM THE BEST

At a Berkshire Hathaway meeting not long ago, Buffett and Munger were asked about the possibility that their two great minds would educate a new generation of investors. That, of course, is exactly what they have both been doing for the past twenty years. Berkshire Hathaway's annual reports are famous for their clarity, absence of mumbo jumbo, and superb educational value. Anyone fortunate enough to attend a Berkshire Hathaway annual meeting knows how illuminating they can be.

(Those who cannot be there in person can gain the benefit of Buffett's and Munger's remarks, along with other speeches and interviews, as ably reported in Henry Emerson's *Outstanding Investor Digest*.) By their example and their public words, Warren Buffett and Charlie Munger have helped teach many thousands of investors how to think about the process of investing, just as they in turn learned from their teachers.

One thing we know about Charlie is that he "believes in the discipline of mastering the best that other people have figured out. I don't believe in just sitting down and trying to dream it all up yourself. Nobody's that smart." (OID)[29]

Buffett would agree. "I've mainly learned by reading myself," he said. "So I don't think I have any original ideas. Certainly, I talk about reading Graham. I've read Phil Fisher. So I've gotten a lot of ideas myself from reading." According to Buffett, "You can learn a lot from other people. In fact, I think if you learn basically from other people, you don't have to get too many new ideas on your own. You can just apply the best of what you see." (OID)[30]

Gaining knowledge is a journey. Warren Buffett and Charlie Munger took much of their wisdom from people who came before them, shaped it into their own mosaic of understanding, and now generously offer it to others—that is, to others who are willing to do their own homework and learn all they can, with a fresh, vigorous, open mind.

"It's extraordinary how resistant some people are to learning anything," Charlie once said. "What's really astounding," Buffett added, "is how resistant they are even when it's in their self-interest to learn." Then, in a more reflective tone, Buffett continued, "There is just an incredible resistance to thinking or changing. I quoted Bertrand Russell one time, saying, 'Most men would rather die than think. Many have.' And in a financial sense, that's very true." (OID)[31]

APPENDIX A

Tables A.1 through A.10 display Berkshire Hathaway's common stock portfolios from 1988 through 1997. Chapter 3 discusses the purchase of Coca-Cola stock as an example of Buffett's "big bets." You may also find it interesting to track the distributions of the other holdings.

Table A.1 Berkshire Hathaway 1988 Common Stock Portfolio

Number of Shares	Company	Cost	Market Value	Percentage of Portfolio (%)	Yearly Return (%)	Weighted Return (%)	Equally Weighted Return (%)	2% Weighted Return (%)
3,000,000	Capital Cities/ABC, Inc.	$ 517,500.00	$1,086,750.00	35.6	5.1	1.8	1.0	0.1
6,850,000	GEICO Corporation	45,713.00	849,400.00	27.8	13.5	3.8	2.7	0.3
14,172,500	The Coca-Cola Company	592,540.00	632,448.00	20.7	22.8	4.7	4.6	0.5
1,727,765	The Washington Post Company	9,731.00	364,126.00	11.9	13.6	1.6	2.7	0.3
2,400,000	Federal Home Loan Mortgage	71,729.00	121,200.00	4.0		0.0	0.0	0.0
	Total common stocks	$1,237,213.00	$3,053,924.00	100.0		11.9	11.0	14.9*
						S&P 500 Return	16.6%	16.0

Source of data: Berkshire Hathaway 1988 Annual Report.

Note: Dollar amounts are in thousands.

*Market return (S&P 500) represents 90% of portfolio.

Table A.2 Berkshire Hathaway 1989 Common Stock Portfolio

Number of Shares	Company	Cost	Market Value	Percentage of Portfolio (%)	Yearly Return (%)	Weighted Return (%)	Equally Weighted Return (%)	2% Weighted Return (%)
23,350,000	The Coca-Cola Company	$1,023,920.00	$1,803,787.00	34.8	77.0	26.8	15.4	1.5
3,000,000	Capital Cities/ABC, Inc.	517,500.00	1,692,375.00	32.6	55.8	18.2	11.2	1.1
6,850,000	GEICO Corporation	45,713.00	1,044,625.00	20.1	24.2	4.9	4.8	0.5
1,727,765	The Washington Post Company	9,731.00	486,366.00	9.4	34.6	3.2	6.9	0.7
2,400,000	Federal Home Loan Mortgage	71,729.00	161,100.00	3.1	0.0	0.0	0.0	0.0
								28.5*
	Total Common Stocks	$1,668,593.00	$5,188,253.00	100.0		53.1	38.3	32.3
					S&P 500 Return			31.6%

Source of data: Berkshire Hathaway 1989 Annual Report.

Note: Dollar amounts are in thousands.

*Market return (S&P 500) represents 90% of portfolio.

Table A.3 Berkshire Hathaway 1990 Common Stock Portfolio

Number of Shares	Company	Cost	Market Value	Percentage of Portfolio (%)	Yearly Return (%)	Weighted Return (%)	Equally Weighted Return (%)	2% Weighted Return (%)
46,700,000	The Coca-Cola Company	$1,023,920.00	$2,171,550.00	40.2	22.7	9.1	3.8	0.5
3,000,000	Capital Cities/ABC, Inc.	517,500.00	1,377,375.00	25.5	-18.6	-4.7	-3.1	-0.4
6,850,000	GEICO Corporation	45,713.00	1,110,556.00	20.5	7.5	1.5	1.3	0.2
1,727,765	The Washington Post Company	9,731.00	342,097.00	6.3	-28.4	-1.8	-4.7	-0.6
5,000,000	Wells Fargo & Company	289,431.00	289,375.00	5.4	-16.8	-0.9	-2.8	-0.3
2,400,000	Federal Home Loan Mortgage	71,729.00	117,000.00	2.2	-25.4	-0.6	-4.2	-0.5
								-2.7*
	Total Common Stocks	$1,958,024.00	$5,407,953.00	100.0		2.7	-9.8	-3.9
					S&P 500 Return			-3.1%

Source of data: Berkshire Hathaway 1990 Annual Report.

Note: Dollar amounts are in thousands.

*Market return (S&P 500) represents 88% of portfolio.

Table A.4 Berkshire Hathaway 1991 Common Stock Portfolio

Number of Shares	Company	Cost	Market Value	Percentage of Portfolio (%)	Yearly Return (%)	Weighted Return (%)	Equally Weighted Return (%)	2% Weighted Return (%)
46,700,000	The Coca-Cola Company	$1,023,920.00	$3,747,675.00	42.9	75.4	32.4	10.8	1.5
6,850,000	GEICO Corporation	45,713.00	1,363,150.00	15.6	23.8	3.7	3.4	0.5
24,000,000	The Gillette Company	600,000.00	1,347,000.00	15.4	81.8	12.6	11.7	1.6
3,000,000	Capital Cities/ABC, Inc.	517,500.00	1,300,500.00	14.9	−5.5	−0.8	−0.8	−0.1
2,495,200	Federal Home Loan Mortgage	77,245.00	343,090.00	3.9	188.0	7.4	26.9	3.8
1,727,765	The Washington Post Company	9,731.00	336,050.00	3.9	0.2	0.0	0.0	0.0
5,000,000	Wells Fargo & Company	289,431.00	290,000.00	3.3	5.3	0.2	0.8	0.1
								26.1*
	Total Common Stocks	$2,563,540.00	$8,727,465.00	100.0		55.5	52.7	33.5
						S&P 500 Return		30.4 %

Source of data: Berkshire Hathaway 1991 Annual Report.

Notes: (1) Dollar amounts are in thousands; (2) Does not include Guinness PLC.

*Market return (S&P 500) represents 86% of portfolio.

Table A.5 Berkshire Hathaway 1992 Common Stock Portfolio

Number of Shares	Company	Cost	Market Value	Percentage of Portfolio (%)	Yearly Return (%)	Weighted Return (%)	Equally Weighted Return (%)	2% Weighted Return (%)
93,400,000	The Coca-Cola Company	$1,023,920.00	$ 3,911,125.00	35.1	5.8	2.0	0.7	0.1
34,250,000	GEICO Corporation	45,713.00	2,226,250.00	20.0	64.2	12.8	8.0	1.3
3,000,000	Capital Cities/ABC, Inc.	517,500.00	1,523,500.00	13.7	17.2	2.3	2.1	0.3
24,000,000	The Gillette Company	600,000.00	1,365,000.00	12.3	2.7	0.3	0.3	0.1
16,196,700	Federal Home Loan Mortgage	414,527.00	783,515.00	7.0	7.4	0.5	0.9	0.1
6,358,418	Wells Fargo & Company	380,983.00	485,624.00	4.4	34.5	1.5	4.3	0.7
4,350,000	General Dynamics	312,438.00	450,769.00	4.0	96.7	3.9	12.1	1.9
1,727,765	The Washington Post Company	9,731.00	396,954.00	3.6	20.4	0.7	2.6	0.4
								6.4*
	Total Common Stocks	$3,304,812.00	$11,142,737.00	100.0		24.2	31.1	11.4
						S&P 500 Return		7.6%

Source of data: Berkshire Hathaway 1992 Annual Report.

Notes: (1) Dollar amounts are in thousands; (2) Does not include Guinness PLC.

*Market return (S&P 500) represents 84% of portfolio.

Table A.6 Berkshire Hathaway 1993 Common Stock Portfolio

Number of Shares	Company	Cost	Market Value	Percentage of Portfolio (%)	Yearly Return (%)	Weighted Return (%)	Equally Weighted Return (%)	2% Weighted Return (%)
93,400,000	The Coca-Cola Company	$1,023,920.00	$ 4,167,975.00	37.9	8.3	3.1	1.0	0.2
34,250,000	GEICO Corporation	45,713.00	1,759,594.00	16.0	−19.7	−3.1	−2.5	−0.4
24,000,000	The Gillette Company	600,000.00	1,431,000.00	13.0	6.4	0.8	0.8	0.1
2,000,000	Capital Cities/ABC, Inc.	345,000.00	1,239,000.00	11.3	22.0	2.5	2.8	0.4
6,791,218	Wells Fargo & Company	423,680.00	878,614.00	8.0	73.0	5.8	9.1	1.5
13,654,600	Federal Home Loan Mortgage	307,505.00	681,023.00	6.2	4.9	0.3	0.6	0.1
1,727,765	The Washington Post Company	9,731.00	440,148.00	4.0	12.9	0.5	1.6	0.3
4,350,000	General Dynamics	94,938.00	401,287.00	3.6	48.5	1.8	6.1	1.0
								8.5*
	Total Common Stocks	$2,850,487.00	$10,998,641.00	100.0		11.7	19.5	11.6

S&P 500 Return   10.1%

Source of data: Berkshire Hathaway 1993 Annual Report.

Notes: (1) Dollar amounts are in thousands; (2) Does not include Guinness PLC.

*Market return (S&P 500) represents 84% of portfolio.

Table A.7 Berkshire Hathaway 1994 Common Stock Portfolio

Number of Shares	Company	Cost	Market Value	Percentage of Portfolio (%)	Yearly Return (%)	Weighted Return (%)	Equally Weighted Return (%)	2% Weighted Return (%)
93,400,000	The Coca-Cola Company	$1,023,920.00	$ 5,150,000.00	36.9	17.4	6.4	1.7	0.3
24,000,000	The Gillette Company	600,000.00	1,797,000.00	12.9	27.4	3.5	2.7	0.5
20,000,000	Capital Cities/ABC, Inc.	345,000.00	1,705,000.00	12.2	37.8	4.6	3.8	0.8
34,250,000	Geico Corporation	45,713.00	1,678,250.00	12.0	-2.6	-0.3	-0.3	-0.1
6,791,218	Wells Fargo & Company	423,680.00	984,272.00	7.0	15.2	1.1	1.5	0.3
27,759,941	American Express Company	723,919.00	818,918.00	5.9	12.4	0.7	1.2	0.2
13,654,600	Federal Home Loan Mortgage	270,468.00	644,441.00	4.6	3.2	0.1	0.3	0.1
1,727,765	The Washington Post Company	9,731.00	418,983.00	3.0	-3.2	-0.1	-0.3	-0.1
19,453,300	PNC Bank Corporation	503,046.00	410,951.00	2.9	-23.6	-0.7	-2.4	-0.5
6,854,500	Gannett Co., Inc.	335,216.00	365,002.00	2.6	-4.5	-0.1	-0.5	-0.1
								1.1*
	Total Common Stocks	$4,280,693.00	$13,972,817.00	100.0		15.3	8.0	2.6

S&P 500 Return 1.3 %

Source of data: Berkshire Hathaway 1994 Annual Report.

Note: Dollar amounts are in thousands.

*Market return (S&P 500) represents 80% of portfolio.

Table A.8 Berkshire Hathaway 1995 Common Stock Portfolio

Number of Shares	Company	Cost	Market Value	Percentage of Portfolio (%)	Yearly Return (%)	Weighted Return (%)	Equally Weighted Return (%)	2% Weighted Return (%)
49,456,900	American Express Company	$1,392.70	$ 2,046.30	10.6	42.8	4.5	6.1	0.9
20,000,000	Capital Cities/ABC, Inc.	345.00	2,467.50	12.8	44.9	5.7	6.4	0.9
100,000,000	The Coca-Cola Company	1,298.90	7,425.00	38.4	46.1	17.7	6.6	0.9
12,502,500	Federal Home Loan Mortgage	260.10	1,044.00	5.4	68.2	3.7	9.7	1.4
34,250,000	GEICO Corp.	45.70	2,393.20	12.4	44.1	5.5	6.3	0.9
48,000,000	The Gillette Company	600.00	2,502.00	12.9	41.1	5.3	5.9	0.8
6,791,218	Wells Fargo & Company	423.70	1,466.90	7.6	15.2	1.2	2.2	0.3
	Total Common Stocks	$4,366.10	$19,344.90	100.0		43.6	43.2	32.3 *
					S&P 500 Return			38.3
								37.6 %

Source of data: Berkshire Hathaway 1995 Annual Report.

Note: Dollar amounts are in millions.

*Market return (S&P 500) represents 86% of portfolio.

Table A.9 Berkshire Hathaway 1996 Common Stock Portfolio

Number of Shares	Company	Cost	Market Value	Percentage of Portfolio (%)	Yearly Return (%)	Weighted Return (%)	Equally Weighted Return (%)	2% Weighted Return (%)
49,456,900	American Express Company	$1,392.70	$ 2,794.30	11.4	39.8	4.5	5.0	0.8
200,000,000	The Coca-Cola Company	1,298.90	10,525.00	43.0	43.2	18.6	5.4	0.9
24,614,214	The Walt Disney Company	577.00	1,716.80	7.0	19.1	1.3	2.4	0.4
64,246,000	Federal Home Loan Mortgage	333.40	1,772.80	7.2	34.2	2.5	4.3	0.7
48,000,000	The Gillette Company	600.00	3,732.00	15.3	50.9	7.8	6.4	1.0
30,156,600	McDonald's Corporation	1,265.30	1,368.40	5.6	1.2	0.1	0.1	0.0
1,727,765	The Washington Post Company	10.60	579.00	2.4	20.6	0.5	2.6	0.4
7,291,418	Wells Fargo & Company	497.80	1,966.90	8.0	27.6	2.2	3.4	0.6
								19.3*
	Total Common Stocks	$5,975.70	$24,455.20	100.0		37.5	29.6	24.0
						S&P 500 Return	23.0 %	

Source of data: Berkshire Hathaway 1996 Annual Report.

Note: Dollar amounts are in millions.

*Market return (S&P 500) represents 84% of portfolio.

Table A.10 Berkshire Hathaway 1997 Common Stock Portfolio

Number of Shares	Company	Cost	Market Value	Percentage of Portfolio (%)	Yearly Return (%)	Weighted Return (%)	Equally Weighted Return (%)	2% Weighted Return (%)
49,456,900	American Express Company	$1,392.70	$ 4,414.00	13.9	59.8	8.3	7.5	1.2
200,000,000	The Coca-Cola Company	1,298.90	13,337.50	42.0	27.9	11.7	3.5	0.6
21,563,414	The Walt Disney Company	381.20	2,134.80	6.7	42.8	2.9	5.4	0.9
63,977,600	Freddie Mac	329.40	2,683.10	8.4	53.8	4.5	6.7	1.1
48,000,000	The Gillette Company	600.00	4,821.00	15.2	30.4	4.6	3.8	0.6
23,733,198	Travelers Group Inc.	604.40	1,278.60	4.0	78.8	3.2	9.9	1.6
1,727,765	The Washington Post Company	10.60	840.60	2.6	47.0	1.2	5.9	0.9
6,690,218	Wells Fargo & Company	412.60	2,270.90	7.1	28.2	2.0	3.5	0.6
	Total Common Stocks	$5,029.80	$31,780.50	100.0		38.5	46.1	28.0* ‾‾‾ 35.4
						S&P 500 Return		33.35%

Source of data: Berkshire Hathaway 1997 Annual Report.

Note: Dollar amounts are in millions.

*Market return (S&P 500) represents 84% of portfolio.

APPENDIX B

The 1,200 companies that we tracked for the purpose of constructing hypothetical "focus" portfolios also give us the data we need to investigate the correlation between a company's operating earnings and its share price. We screened the Compustat database, asking for all companies that had values for earnings per share and price for our entire eighteen-year time period (1979–1996). We used price close calendar year and EPS fully diluted excluding extraordinary items. Then we took the resulting 1,200 companies and calculated EPS growth (EPS slope divided by the standard deviation) and price growth (using the geometric average) for the selected time periods. We then plotted EPS growth versus price growth in Excel and asked for the trend line and correlation between the two variables. In Tables B.1 through B.5, the correlations are displayed for four different time periods: five, seven, ten, and eighteen years.

For example, Table B.1 shows the relationship between earnings and the price of our companies measured in three-year time periods. If we take the earnings per share of our 1,200 companies from 1978 through 1980 and compare it against the price behavior of our companies in the three years following (1979–1981), we can see that the correlation between the two variables is rather weak: .275. This suggests that 27 percent of the variance in price was explained by the variation in earnings.

For every three-year period from 1978 through 1995, we can see that the relationship between earnings per share and price is not particularly strong, ranging between a low of .131 and .360. But what happens if we extend the holding period?

Table B.2 shows the relationship between earnings and share price when we hold a stock for five years. The correlation moves higher, ranging between a low of .374 to as high as .599. A seven-year holding period (Table B.3) strengthens the correlation, from .473 to .670. In a ten-year study (Table B.4), the correlation ranges between .593 to .695. And in the eighteen-year holding period (Table B.5), the correlation is .688—a significantly meaningful relationship.

Note that in each table a decline in the relative correlation has occurred over the time period. For example, in Table B.4, the correlation earnings per share and price in 1979–1988 dropped from .688 to .598 during 1987–1996. The slight decline in the relationship between the two variables is attributed not to the breakdown in the corelation but rather to the impact that lower interest rates and lower inflation have had on stock prices. Since 1987, there has been a secular decline in both interest rates and inflation, and this has caused the valuation of stocks to rise significantly, apart from the impact of earnings.

Table B.1 3-Year Data

EPS vs. Price

EPS	Price	Number Companies	Correlation
1978–1980	1979–1981	1200	0.2758772
1979–1981	1980–1982	1200	0.2629829
1980–1982	1981–1983	1200	0.2568294
1981–1983	1982–1984	1200	0.2797025
1982–1984	1983–1985	1200	0.3529048
1983–1985	1984–1986	1200	0.3418487
1984–1986	1985–1987	1200	0.3460620
1985–1987	1986–1988	1200	0.2906888
1986–1988	1987–1989	1200	0.2312670
1987–1989	1988–1990	1200	0.3606748
1988–1990	1989–1991	1200	0.1694468
1989–1991	1990–1992	1200	0.1315295
1990–1992	1991–1993	1200	0.1577973
1991–1993	1992–1994	1200	0.1479865
1992–1994	1993–1995	1200	0.2509980
1993–1995	1994–1996	1200	0.2634388

Table B.2 5-Year Data

EPS vs. Price

EPS	Price	Number Companies	Correlation
1978–1982	1979–1983	1200	0.4338561
1979–1983	1980–1984	1200	0.5417748
1980–1984	1981–1985	1200	0.5997851
1981–1985	1982–1986	1200	0.5704438
1982–1986	1983–1987	1200	0.5862316
1983–1987	1984–1988	1200	0.5683841
1984–1988	1985–1989	1200	0.5074871
1985–1989	1986–1990	1200	0.4973158
1986–1990	1987–1991	1200	0.5093590
1987–1991	1988–1992	1200	0.5467952
1988–1992	1989–1993	1200	0.4038872
1989–1993	1990–1994	1200	0.3861604
1990–1994	1991–1995	1200	0.3751835
1991–1995	1992–1996	1200	0.3747853

Table B.3   7-Year Data

EPS vs. Price

EPS	Price	Number Companies	Correlation
1978–1984	1979–1985	1200	0.6241161
1979–1985	1980–1986	1200	0.6705901
1980–1986	1981–1987	1200	0.6508436
1981–1987	1982–1988	1200	0.6026558
1982–1988	1983–1989	1200	0.5925778
1983–1989	1984–1990	1200	0.5988441
1984–1990	1985–1991	1200	0.6302446
1985–1991	1986–1992	1200	0.6035084
1986–1992	1987–1993	1200	0.5340913
1987–1993	1988–1994	1200	0.5583143
1988–1994	1989–1995	1200	0.4820943
1989–1995	1990–1996	1200	0.4737507

Table B.4   10-Year Data

EPS vs. Price

EPS	Price	Number Companies	Correlation
1978–1987	1979–1988	1200	0.6886247
1979–1988	1980–1989	1200	0.6954808
1980–1989	1981–1990	1200	0.6695781
1981–1990	1982–1991	1200	0.6743078
1982–1991	1983–1992	1200	0.6803716
1983–1992	1984–1993	1200	0.6229406
1984–1993	1985–1994	1200	0.5950414
1985–1994	1986–1995	1200	0.5938911
1986–1995	1987–1996	1200	0.5982626

Table B.5   18-Year Data

EPS vs. Price

EPS	Price	Number Companies	Correlation
1978–1995	1979–1996	1200	0.6889752

NOTES

ONE: **Focus Investing**

Epigraph: Interview, Warren Buffett, August 1994.
1. Andrew Barry, "With Little Cheery News in Sight, Stocks Take a Break," *Barron's*, November 16, 1998, MW1.
2. Berkshire Hathaway Annual Report, 1993, p. 15.
3. Ibid.
4. Berkshire Hathaway Annual Report, 1991, p. 15.
5. Interview with Philip Fisher, September 15, 1998.
6. Philip Fisher, *Common Stocks and Uncommon Profits* (New York: John Wiley & Sons, Inc., 1996), p. 108.
7. Interview with Philip Fisher, September 15, 1998.
8. Interview with Ken Fisher, September 15, 1998.
9. Ibid.
10. Interview with Warren Buffett, August 1994.
11. *Outstanding Investor Digest*, August 10, 1995, p. 63.
12. Ibid.
13. *Outstanding Investor Digest*, May 5, 1995, p. 49.
14. *Outstanding Investor Digest*, August 8, 1997, p. 61.
15. *Outstanding Investor Digest*, August 8, 1997, p. 13.
16. *Outstanding Investor Digest*, June 23, 1994, p. 31.

TWO: **The High Priests of Modern Finance**

Epigraph: Widely quoted remark.
1. For a comprehensive and well written historical recovery of the development of modern finance, see: Peter Bernstein, *Capital Ideas: The Improbable Origins of Modern Wall Street* (New York: The Free Press, 1992).
2. Ibid, p. 47.
3. Jonathan Burton, "Travels Along the Efficient Frontier," *Dow Jones Asset Management*, May/June 1997, p. 22.
4. Bernstein, p. 86.

5. Ibid, p. 13.
6. *Outstanding Investor Digest,* April 18, 1990, p. 18.
7. Berkshire Hathaway Annual Report, 1993, p. 13.
8. "Intrinsic value risk" is a term first coined by John Rutledge of Rutledge & Company, Greenwich, CT, *Forbes,* August 29, 1994, p. 279.
9. Berkshire Hathaway Annual Report, 1993, p. 13.
10. *Outstanding Investor Digest,* June 23, 1994, p. 19.
11. Berkshire Hathaway Annual Report, 1993, p. 13.
12. Berkshire Hathaway Annual Report, 1993, p. 12.
13. *Outstanding Investor Digest,* August 8, 1996, p. 29.
14. Berkshire Hathaway Annual Report, 1988, p. 18.
15. Ibid.
16. Benjamin Graham, *The Intelligent Investor: A Book of Practical Counsel* (New York: Harper & Row, 1973), p. 287.

THREE: The Superinvestors of Buffettville

Epigraph: *Fortune,* 1989.
1. Benjamin Graham, *The Memoirs of the Dean of Wall Street* (New York: McGraw-Hill, 1996), p. 239.
2. The speech was adapted as an article in the Columbia Business School's publication *Hermes* (Fall 1984), with the same title. The remarks directly quoted here are from that article.
3. Buffett, "The Superinvestors of Graham-and-Doddsville," *Hermes* (Fall 1984). The superinvestors Buffett presented in the article included Walter Schloss, who worked at Graham-Newman Corporation in the mid-1950s, along with Buffett; Tom Knapp, another Graham-Newman alumnus, who later formed Tweedy-Browne Partners with Ed Anderson, also a Graham follower; Bill Ruane, a former Graham student who went on to establish the Sequoia Fund; Buffett's partner Charlie Munger; Rick Guerin of Pacific Partners; and Stan Perlmeter of Perlmeter Investments.
4. Jess H. Chua and Richard S. Woodward, "J.M. Keynes's Investment Performances: A Note." *The Journal of Finance,* Vol. XXXVIII, No.1, March 1983.
5. Ibid.
6. Ibid.
7. Buffett, "Superinvestors."
8. Ibid.
9. Ibid.

10. Sequoia Fund Annual Report, 1996.
11. Solveig Jansson, "GEICO Sticks to Its Last," *Institutional Investor,* July 1986, p. 130.
12. Berkshire Hathaway Annual Report, 1986, p. 15.
13. Berkshire Hathaway Annual Report, 1995, p. 10.
14. Ibid.
15. Ibid.
16. The research described here is part of a larger research study I conducted with Joan Lamm-Tennant, PhD, Vice-President, General Re Corporation, Stamford, Connecticut. Our findings are described in a monograph titled "Focus Investing: An Alternative to Active Management versus Indexing."
17. It is important to note that when the benchmark return is higher than the median return of the broadly diversified portfolio, the probabilities of outperforming the benchmark rise to the degree the portfolio manager is willing to reduce the number of stocks in the portfolio. If the benchmark return is less than the median return of the broadly diversified portfolio, this relationship does not hold. In other words, a group of concentrated portfolios under this circumstance would not have more probabilities of outperforming the benchmark, compared to a group of broadly diversified portfolios. However, the group of concentrated portfolios still gives the potential for higher returns when compared against a group of broadly diversified portfolios.
18. Buffett, "Superinvestors."
19. Buffett, "Superinvestors."

FOUR: A Better Way to Measure Performance

Epigraph: Warren Buffett, "The Superinvestors of Graham-and-Doddsville," *Hermes* (Fall 1984).
1. Joseph Nocera, "Who's Got the Answers?" *Fortune,* November 24, 1997, p. 329.
2. Ibid.
3. Eugene Shahan, "Are Short-Term Performance and Value Investing Mutually Exclusive?" *Hermes* (Spring 1986).
4. Sequoia Fund, Quarterly Report, March 31, 1996.
5. Mark Carhart, "On Persistence in Mutual Fund Performance," *The Journal of Finance,* Vol. LII, No. 1, March 1997; Burton G. Malkiel, "Returns from Investing in Equity Mutual Funds 1971 to 1991," *The Journal of Finance,* Vol. L, No. 2, June 1995.

6. Darryll Hendricks, Jayendu Patel, and Richard Zeckhauser, "Hot Hands in Mutual Funds: Short-Run Persistence of Relative Performance, 1974–1988," *The Journal of Finance,* Vol. XLVIII, No. 1, March 1993.
7. Stephen J. Brown and William N. Goetzmann, "Performance Persistence," *The Journal of Finance,* Vol. L, No. 2, June 1995.
8. Widely used quote by Warren Buffett.
9. Berkshire Hathaway Annual Report, 1987, p. 14.
10. Ibid.
11. Ibid.
12. Berkshire Hathaway Annual Report, 1981, p. 39.
13. Benjamin Graham, *Security Analysis* (New York: McGraw-Hill, 1951).
14. Berkshire Hathaway Annual Report, 1987, p. 15.
15. Berkshire Hathaway Annual Report, 1991, p. 8.
16. Ibid.
17. *Outstanding Investor Digest,* August 10, 1995, p. 10.
18. Ibid.
19. Widely quoted by Tom Murphy. Train metaphor used to describe how to manage a holding company.
20. Berkshire Hathaway Annual Report, 1996.
21. Ibid.
22. Carole Gould, "The Price of Turnover," *The New York Times,* November 21, 1997.
23. Robert Jeffrey and Robert Arnott, "Is Your Alpha Big Enough to Cover Your Taxes?" *Journal of Portfolio Management,* Spring 1993.
24. Ibid.
25. Ibid.
26. *Outstanding Investor Digest,* May 5, 1995, p. 61.
27. Peter Bernstein, "Immortal Words—Impossible," *The Journal of Portfolio Management,* Summer 1995, p. 1.
28. *Outstanding Investor Digest,* May 5, 1998.

FIVE: **The Warren Buffett Way Tool Belt**

Epigraph: *The Commercial and Financial Chronicle,* December 6, 1951.
1. *Outstanding Investor Digest,* August 8, 1997, p. 14.
2. Ibid.
3. Ibid., p. 18.
4. Ibid., p. 17.
5. *Outstanding Investor Digest,* August 8, 1996, p. 34.
6. Berkshire Hathaway Annual Meeting, 1995.

7. Berkshire Hathaway Annual Report, 1992, pp. 13–14.
8. Ibid.
9. *Outstanding Investor Digest,* August 8, 1996, p. 29.
10. "Will the Real Ben Graham Please Stand Up?" *Forbes,* December 11, 1989, p. 310.
11. Interview with Eric Savitz, December 2, 1998.
12. Interview with Amy Arnott, December 2, 1998.
13. Adam Shell, "Bill Miller: Beating the Market Is Routine," *Investor's Business Daily,* November 7, 1997.
14. James Cramer, "Wrong! Rear Echelon Revelations: Mutual Funds and Value Judgements," *TheStreet.com,* July 27, 1998.
15. Sandra Ward, "Another Legend, Another Book?" *Barron's,* June 22, 1998, p. 44.
16. *Outstanding Investor Digest,* September 24, 1998, p. 48.
17. *Outstanding Investor Digest,* March 13, 1998, p. 55.
18. Ibid.
19. Interview with Bill Miller, December 1, 1998.
20. A reference book that Bill Miller often cites as insightful to the process of understanding technology companies is: Jeff Moone, *The Gorilla Game: An Investor's Guide to Picking Winners in High Technology* (New York: HarperCollins Publishers, 1998).
21. Interview with Lisa Rapuano, December 2, 1998.
22. Interview with Bill Miller, December 1, 1998.
23. Ibid.
24. Interview with Michael Mauboussin, December 2, 1998.
25. Ibid.

six: The Mathematics of Investing

Epigraph: *Outstanding Investor Digest,* June 23, 1994, p. 19.
1. For an excellent read of Warren Buffett's life, see Roger Lowenstein's, *Buffett: The Making of an American Capitalist* (New York: Random House, 1995).
2. Alexander Alger, "Buffett on Bridge," *Forbes,* June 2, 1997, pp. 206–207.
3. Andrew Kilpatrick, *Of Permanent Value: The Story of Warren Buffett,* p. 533. Quotes from Chris Stavrou's meeting with Warren Buffett are cited here (Birmingham, AL: AKPE Publisher, 1998).
4. *Outstanding Investor Digest,* May 5, 1995, p. 49.
5. Peter L. Bernstein, *Against the Gods* (New York: John Wiley & Sons, Inc., 1996), p. 63.

6. Ibid.
7. Ibid.
8. *Outstanding Investor Digest,* May 5, 1995, p. 49.
9. Robert L. Winkler, *An Introduction to Bayesian Inference and Decision* (New York: Holt, Rinehart and Winston, 1972), p. 17.
10. Kilpatrick, *Of Permanent Value: The Story of Warren Buffett,* p. 800.
11. *Outstanding Investor Digest,* April 18, 1990, p. 16.
12. Ibid.
13. Ibid.
14. *Outstanding Investor Digest,* June 23, 1994, p. 19.
15. Robert G. Hagstrom Jr., *The Warren Buffett Way* (New York: John Wiley & Sons, Inc., 1994).
16. Berkshire Hathaway Annual Report, 1990, p. 16.
17. Ibid.
18. Berkshire Hathaway Annual Report, 1993, p. 16.
19. Berkshire Hathaway Annual Report, 1993, p. 15.
20. Edward O. Thorp, *Beat the Dealer: A Winning Strategy for the Game of Twenty-One* (New York: Vintage Books, 1962).
21. I am indebted to William H. Miller III for pointing out the J.L. Kelly growth model.
22. C.E. Shannon, "A Mathematical Theory of Communication," *The Bell System Technical Journal,* Vol. XXVII, No. 3, July 1948.
23. J.L. Kelly Jr., "A New Interpretation of Information Rate," *The Bell System Technical Journal,* Vol. XXXV, No. 3, July 1956.
24. Interview with Ed Thorp, November 25, 1998.
25. *Outstanding Investor Digest,* August 8, 1996, p. 23.
26. Berkshire Hathaway Annual Report, 1992, p. 11.
27. Berkshire Hathaway Annual Report, 1996, p. 9.
28. Ibid.
29. Interview with Ajit Jain, December 15, 1998.
30. Interview with Charlie Munger, May 1997.
31. Berkshire Hathaway Annual Report, 1997, p. 8.
32. Berkshire Hathaway Annual Report, 1995, p. 13.
33. *Outstanding Investor Digest,* May 5, 1995, p. 57.
34. Ibid.
35. Andrew Beyer, *Picking Winners, A Horse Player's Guide* (New York: Houghton Mifflin Company, 1994), p. 178.
36. *Outstanding Investor Digest,* December 29, 1997, p. 30.
37. *Outstanding Investor Digest,* May 5, 1995, p. 58.
38. Ibid., p. 50.
39. Ibid.
40. Berkshire Hathaway Annual Report, 1996, p. 15.

SEVEN: **The Psychology of Investing**

Epigraph: Andrew Kilpatrick, *Of Permanent Value: The Story of Warren Buffett* (Birmingham, AL: AKPE Publisher, 1998), p. 683.

1. *Outstanding Investor Digest,* August 10, 1995, p. 11.
2. Benjamin Graham, *The Intelligent Investor: A Book of Practical Counsel* (New York: Harper & Row, 1973), p. 106.
3. Ibid., p. 107.
4. Fuerbringer, "Why Both Bulls and Bears Can Act So Bird-Brained," *The New York Times,* March 30, 1997, section 3, p. 6.
5. *Outstanding Investor Digest,* May 5, 1995, p. 51.
6. Fuerbringer.
7. Brian O'Reilly, "Why Can't Johnny Invest?" *Fortune,* November 9, 1998, p. 73.
8. Jonathan Burton, "It Just Ain't Rational," *Fee Advisor,* September/October 1996, p. 26.
9. Fuerbringer.
10. D.G. Pruitt, "The Walter Mitty Effect in Individual and Good Risk Taking," *Proceedings of the 77th Annual Convention of the American Psychological Association 4* (1969), pp. 425–436.
11. J.W. Atkinson, R. Bastian, W. Earl, and G.H. Litwin, "The Achievement Motive and Goal Setting, and Probability Preference," *Journal of Abnormal and Social Psychology,* 60 (November 1960), pp. 27–36.
J.W. Atkinson, and G.H. Litwin, "The Achievement Motive and Test Anxiety Conceived as a Motive to Avoid Failure," *Journal of Abnormal and Social Psychology,* 60 (November 1960), pp. 52–63.
12. L.W. Littig, "Effects of Skill and Chance Orientation on Probability Preferences," *Psychological Reports, 10* (1962), pp. 72–80.
13. Kilpatrick, p. 683.

EIGHT: **The Market as a Complex System**

Epigraph: Berkshire Hathaway Annual Report, 1992, p. 6.
1. Simon Reynolds, *Thoughts of Chairman Buffett: Thirty Years of Unc-on-ventional Wisdom from the Sage of Omaha* (New York: HarperCollins, 1998).
2. Michael Mauboussin, "Shift Happens: On a New Paradigm of the Markets as a Complex Adaptive System," *Frontiers of Finance,* October 24, 1997.
3. Dr. Roger White, "Chaos and Complexity" (Knowledge Products: Carmichael and Carmichael, Inc.), 1993.

4. Ibid.

5. Mitchel M. Waldrop, *Complexity: The Emerging Science at the Edge of Order and Chaos* (New York: Simon & Schuster, 1992), p. 335.

6. Ibid.

7. Ibid.

8. Ibid.

9. W.B. Arthur, S.N. Durlauf, and D. Lane, "Process and Emergence in the Economy," *The Economy as an Evolving Complex System II* (Reading, MA: Addison-Wesley), 1997, p. 1.

10. John Casti, "What If," *The New Scientist,* July 13, 1996, p. 36.

11. Andrew Barry, "Trigger-Happy," *Barron's,* December 8, 1997, p. 21.

12. John M. Keynes, *The General Theory of Employment, Interest and Money* (New York: A Harvest Book, 1964), p. 156.

13. Berkshire Hathaway Annual Report, 1987, p. 17.

14. Gordon Arnaut, "Marketing 'Flight Simulators' for Business," *The New York Times,* December 8, 1997, p. D4.

15. Casti, p. 38.

16. Ibid.

17. Interview with Michael Mauboussin, December 2, 1998.

18. Michael Mauboussin, "On the Shoulders of Giants," *Frontiers of Strategy,* Vol. 2, Crédit Suisse First Boston, November 16, 1998.

19. Interview with Michael Mauboussin.

20. Loren Fleckenstein, "Fund Manager Embraces Complexity," *Investor's Business Daily,* May 14, 1998.

21. Ibid.

22. Diane Banegas, "Mutual Fund Manager Bill Miller Sees Value in the Business Network," *SFI Bulletin,* Winter 1998.

23. Ibid.

24. Ibid.

25. Interview with Bill Miller, December 1, 1998.

26. Fleckenstein.

27. Fleckenstein, "Don't Dwell on Why the Market Moves," *Investor's Business Daily,* October 15, 1998.

28. Ibid.

29. George Johnson, *Fire in the Mind: Science, Faith, and the Search for Order* (New York: Vintage Books, 1995), p. 104.

30. Waldrop, p. 334.

31. Andrew Kilpatrick, *Of Permanent Value: The Story of Warren Buffett* (Birmingham, AL: AKPE Publisher, 1998), p. 794.

32. Berkshire Hathaway Annual Report, 1994, p. 1.

33. Ibid.

34. Ibid.

35. *Forbes,* Vol. 124, No. 3., August 6, 1979, pp. 25, 26.

NINE: **Where Are the .400 Hitters?**

Epigraph: Ted Williams, *The Science of Hitting* (New York: Simon & Schuster, 1986), p. 24.

  1. Stephen Jay Gould, *Full House: The Spread of Excellence from Plato to Darwin* (New York: Crown, 1996), p. 116.

  2. Peter Bernstein, "Where, Oh Where Are the .400 Hitters of Yesteryear?" *Financial Analysts Journal,* November/December 1998, p. 6.

  3. Ibid., p. 11.

  4. *Broadcasting* magazine, June 9, 1996. See Simon Reynolds, *Thoughts of Chairman Buffett: Thirty Years of Unconventional Wisdom from the Sage of Omaha* (New York: HarperCollins, 1998).

  5. Berkshire Hathaway Annual Report, 1996. p. 16.

  6. Berkshire Hathaway Annual Report, 1987, p. 14.

  7. Berkshire Hathaway Annual Report, 1996, p. 16.

  8. *Outstanding Investor Digest,* April 18, 1990, p. 17.

  9. Ronald Surz, "R-Squareds and Alphas Are Far from Different Alphabets," *The Journal of Investing,* Summer 1998.

10. Berkshire Hathaway Annual Report, 1983, p. 14.

11. *Outstanding Investor Digest,* May 5, 1995, p. 51.

12. S.J. Simon, *Why You Lose at Bridge* (Louisville, KY: Devyn Press, Inc., 1994), p. 9.

13. *Outstanding Investor Digest,* August 8, 1996, p. 39.

14. *Outstanding Investor Digest,* May 5, 1995, p. 51.

15. Ibid.

16. *Outstanding Investor Digest,* March 13, 1998, p. 56.

17. *Outstanding Investor Digest,* August 8, 1997, p. 19.

18. Berkshire Hathaway Annual Report, 1997, p. 5.

19. Ibid.

20. A frequently quoted statement from Warren Buffett.

21. *Outstanding Investor Digest,* August 8, 1997, p. 15.

22. *Outstanding Investor Digest,* September 24, 1998, p. 40.

23. Thomas S. Kuhn, *The Structure of Scientific Revolutions* (Chicago: The University of Chicago Press, 1970), p. 77.

24. John Maynard Keynes, *The General Theory of Employment, Interest, and Money* (Orlando, FL: Harcourt Brace & Company, 1964).

25. Benjamin Graham and David Dodd, *Security Analysis* (New York: McGraw-Hill Book Company, 1951).

26. *Outstanding Investor Digest,* August 8, 1997, p. 14.

27. I am indebted to Bob Coleman and Larry Pidgeon for thoughts on this subject.

28. Ron Chernow, *The Death of the Banker: The Decline and Fall of the Great Financial Dynasties and the Triumph of the Small Investor* (New York: Vintage Books, 1997).

29. *Outstanding Investor Digest,* March 13, 1998, p. 63.

30. *Outstanding Investor Digest,* August 10, 1995, p. 21.

31. *Outstanding Investor Digest,* August 10, 1995, p. 21.

ACKNOWLEDGMENTS

I have studied Warren Buffett for over fifteen years. During that period, I have had the opportunity to observe one of the greatest investors in history. I have also had the opportunity to exchange ideas and work with many talented individuals who, in their own way, have made me not only a better writer and investor, but a better person.

I would like first of all to thank Warren Buffett for his teachings and for allowing me to use his copyrighted material. It is impossible to improve what Mr. Buffett has already said. The readers of this book are fortunate to be able to read his own words rather than be subjected to a second-best paraphrase.

Thanks also to Charlie Munger. In *The Warren Buffett Way*, I underemphasized the importance of Charlie not only to Berkshire Hathaway but to the lessons he has taught investors around the world. His "latticework of models" approach to achieving worldly wisdom is destined to become a classic.

We owe a special debt of gratitude to *Outstanding Investor Digest*. Widely known as OID, *Outstanding Investor Digest* is an exceptional publication that provides individuals the opportunity to hear some of the best ideas from some of the top money managers in the country. In addition, OID covers Berkshire Hathaway's annual meetings as well as an occasional lecture given by Warren Buffett and Charlie Munger. In this book, I have included numerous quotations which have been incorporated with their permission. These quotations, which are designated by OID in parentheses, will give readers a first-person insight on focus investing as well as the psychology of investing. If you have not had an opportunity to read OID, do yourself a favor and look them up at www.oid.com or give them a call at 212-925-3885. I don't believe you will be disappointed.

Thanks also to Andy Kilpatrick, author of *Of Permanent Value: The Story of Warren Buffett.* Any time I need a refresher on Buffett or Berkshire Hathaway, I turn to Andy's book. He is, in my judgment, the official historian of Berkshire Hathaway.

Several people took their valuable time to read the manuscript and offer suggestions. I wish to thank Bill Ruane, Lou Simpson, Phil Fisher, Bob Coleman, Tom Russo, and Michael Mauboussin.

Several others offered their expert opinion for portions of the book. I have benefited from Ajit Jain at Berkshire Hathaway and Alice Schroeder at Paine Webber; both helped me better understand super-catastrophe insurance underwriting. Ed Thorp, PhD, and Michael Levitan, PhD, patiently tutored me on statistical probabilities.

I was fortunate to be able to work with Joan Lamm-Tennant, PhD, Vice President of General Re, as we both studied intensely the concept of focus investing. Thanks also to Pat Shunk for his computer programming assistance.

I owe a special debt of gratitude to William H. Miller III, president of Legg Mason Fund Adviser and portfolio manager of the Legg Mason Value Trust. Bill has been a friend and intellectual coach of mine for many years now. Many of you know he was helpful to me when I wrote *The Warren Buffett Way.* This time, he was even more generous; he diligently read each page of the manuscript and then offered valuable suggestions. What is particularly exciting for me is that Bill is not only a friend and teacher, he is now a colleague.

Everyone at Legg Mason Fund Adviser has welcomed Focus Capital with open arms and endless support. We owe many thanks to Nancy Dennin, Lisa Rapuano, David Nelson, Ernie Kiehne, Kyle Legg, Mary Chris Gay, Jay Leopold, Randy Befumo, Chip Coleman, Michael Ray, Burr Burker, Darlene Orange, Corinne Ratliff, Cassandra Green, and Jennifer Murphy.

At Legg Mason Focus Capital, I wish to thank Tracy Haslett for her help in preparing the manuscript, and Cathy Coladonato who works hard to keep our firm running smoothly. Special thanks to Ericka Merluzzi, my research assistant. Ericka's research and investigation have always been first class. Her work at Focus Capital is invaluable.

My relationship with John Wiley & Sons, Inc., has been outstanding. I wish to thank my publisher and friend Myles Thompson for his continued support. Thanks also to Jennifer Pincott, associate editor; to Mary Daniello, associate managing editor; and to Nancy Marcus Land and Maryan Malone at Publications Development Company, for editorial expertise.

I am greatly indebted to Laurie Harper at Sebastian Literary Agency. Laurie is a perfect agent. She is smart and loyal, and, in all aspects of work, acts with a high level of integrity. She is, in a word, special.

I want to express my deep appreciation to my cowriter, Maggie Stuckey of Portland, Oregon. This is the third book Maggie and I have written together, and I can tell you honestly that, many times, I would have given up without her. Even though we work at opposite ends of the continent, Maggie has a special gift of connecting intimately with the work I get started. Somehow she gets inside my brain and knows what I want to say even before I do, and helps me say it better. Maggie Stuckey is the best in the business, and I am fortunate that she has chosen to share her talents with me.

So many people have generously given their time and attention to this book. For everything that is right about the book, I thank them. I, alone, am responsible for any mistakes and omissions.

Any writer who is both a parent and a spouse knows the sacrifice one's family must give in order that a book be written. For all the times I said I couldn't play with my sons Robert and John, the answer now is an enthusiastic YES. For all the times I had to lean on my daughter to help out around the house: Kim, you're now off the hook. For my beautiful Maggie, who never complained when she was pulling double duty, I'm back and I love you!

R. G. H.

INDEX